The Future is in Your Hands

Palm Reading Made Easy

The Future is in Your Hands

Palm Reading Made Easy

Cheiro - William J. Warner
Revised and Updated by Irene McGarvie

First Published in 1916 as
"Palmistry For All"

Ancient Wisdom Publishing
a division of Nixon-Carre Ltd., Toronto, ON

Library and Archives Canada Cataloguing in Publication

Cheiro, 1866-1936
        The future is in your hands : palm reading made easy / Cheiro - William H. Warner ; revised and updated by Irene McGarvie.

Includes index.
"First published in 1916 as Palmistry for all".
ISBN 978-0-9783939-8-4

        1. Palmistry. I. McGarvie, Irene, 1957- II. Title.

BF921.C54 2009   133.6   C2009-906649-1

Published by: Ancient Wisdom Publishing
A division of Nixon-Carre Ltd.
P.O. Box 92533 Carlton RPO
Toronto, Ontario, M5A 4N9

www.learnancientwisdom.com
www.nixon-carre.com

Distributed by Ingram 1-800-937-8000
www.ingrambook.com

Printed and bound in the USA

Contents

"Never let the future disturb you.
You will meet it, if you have to,
with the same weapons of reason
which today arm you against the present."

Marcus Aurelius Antoninus
121 A.D. - 180 A.D.
Roman Emperor

Who Was Cheiro?

William John Warner (November 1, 1866 - October 8, 1936) was a famous occult figure of the early 20th century. A lecturer and author, he was known professionally as Cheiro (derived from the word cheiromancy - meaning palmistry).

He was a palm reader, astrologer and clairvoyant who also went by the name Count Louis Hamon, claiming to be the illegitimate son of Count William de Hamon. But this claim was never proven and was more likely just a part of the flamboyant public persona he created to impress his wealthy clients. Born near Dublin Ireland, he traveled extensively throughout his early life, spending a number of years in India where he learned cheiromancy by studying ancient Hindu texts.

He wrote many books on a wide variety of occult topics and his writings form the basis of much of what is known today about the art and science of palm reading. This book is a compilation of his years of study into the art of palmistry.

His ability to judge a person's character through an examination of their hands was uncanny, and his predictions regarding the future were often startlingly accurate. For example, he used a combination of palmistry and other occult techniques to predict the date of Queen Victoria's death, and the year and month when King Edward VII would pass away.

The last years of his life were spent in Hollywood California where he had a huge following of celebrity clients such as Mark Twain, Sarah Bernhardt, Oscar Wilde, and Thomas Edison.

Irene McGarvie
Toronto, Ontario
November, 2009

Introduction

Cheiromancy vs. Cheirognomy

This book endeavors to give the reader a basic understanding of both Cheiromancy (the study of the Lines of the Palm), and Cheirognomy (the study of the shape of the hands and fingers).

Gain an advantage in business

This study is invaluable when it comes to business dealings, and also in endeavoring to ascertain the character of employees. To a judge of horseflesh the limbs of the horse give such a fund of information as to the animal's breed, training, etc., that it enables one to draw conclusions that could not otherwise be obtained. In the same way, the shape of the hand gives an enormous wealth of information as to the peculiarities of human beings.

Although work and exercise may enlarge and broaden the hand, the type to which it belongs is never changed, but can be easily detected by anyone who has made a study of such matters.

Everyone knows that "the face can wear a mask," that a person may be a good actor and put on a certain expression that may deceive even the best judgment. But hands cannot change as the result of a mere effort to please; the character they express is the real nature of the individual -- the true character that has been formed by heredity or that has grown up with the person by long years of habit. Through the use of this information, a mere glance at a hand can give one a quick grasp of the leading characteristics of the persons with whom they are thrown into contact.

Understanding your children

I think that if all parents knew something of this science, the talents of their children would be more usefully developed. It is often too late when a child discovers--and most probably by accident--some tendency or talent that had never been suspected by its parents.

It is no wonder that so few persons find their true vocations in the world, considering the random, haphazard way in which children are brought up--educated for the most part in some scholastic mill that grinds down all to the same level of mediocrity, and then turns them into the army, the church, or into trade.

If, on the contrary, all these studies that teach the understanding of character were more encouraged, parents would have less excuse for the ignorance they show as to the real nature of the children who hold them responsible for their entry into the battlefield of existence.

These same parents would lift up their voices in

righteous indignation if soldiers were sent into battle untrained, without their proper equipment, and yet these same parents have never made the simplest study of any one of those many subjects by which they could, in knowing the nature of their child, have strengthened weak points in their character, or by developing some talent or gift, doubly armed them for their entry into the battle of life.

Study as many hands as possible

I would strongly advise students of this subject to study as many hands as possible and make impressions of the hands in order to make a library or collection, both for their own private study, and also as a valuable record of their work.

Before I read any hands professionally, I had some thousands of casts, impressions on paper, and photographs of hands in my possession, and I found that I derived the most valuable aid from being able to analyze and study their shapes and markings at my leisure.

The best means of taking these impressions is to obtain a small roller used by printers for fine work, such as die stamping, a tube of printer's ink, and a small sheet of glass to roll the ink out until it covers the surface of the roller in an even way.

The roller may then be passed over the surface of the palm, the hand pressed firmly down on a smooth sheet of white paper, and with a little practice, excellent impressions can easily be obtained.

When the impression is dry it can be dated, numbered,

and placed in an album for reference.

Editor's note: This book was originally written in 1916, today's student of palmistry has a much easier method of making impressions through the use of the photocopier or scanner.

The best time for examining hands is during the day, first because the light is better and, above all, because the circulation of the blood does not redden the entire palm as it does at night, and the finer lines can consequently more easily be detected.

The right and left hands should be examined together to note what difference there may be in the shape and position of the lines, but the markings on the dominant hand are the only ones to be relied on.

Lastly, do not be forever on the lookout for faults and failings in the subject whose hands you may be examining, remember no one is perfect, and that faults and failings may in the end be as stepping stones by which we rise to higher things.

Cheiro
Hollywood, California
1916

The Study of the Shape of the Hands

1

Cheirognomy

A quick glance at the shape of a person's hand can give you an indication of their personality and abilities. The study of the shapes of the hands, and fingers is called Cheirognomy from the Greek word cheir meaning hand.

The primary difficulty that most students of Cheirognomy have is in accurately categorizing the shape of the hand. Is the hand elemental or square? The differences in appearance can seem very subtle to the beginner, but the differences in interpretation are huge.

Hands, hard and soft

Even in the simple act of shaking hands, one can form conclusions about character.

Beware of any man or woman whose hand seems to slip from yours when you grasp theirs in greeting. Such persons are deceptive and treacherous. They may smile at you with their lips, but instinctively they regard you as their prey and will only use you for their own ends.

A man or woman, who gives a good firm grasp of the hand, is self-confident, energetic, and generally reliable.

A soft, fat hand is an indication of a lazy person, while a firm hand is the sign of an energetic, reliable nature. A very thin hand denotes a restless energetic disposition, but one that is given to worry and fretting, and is generally discontented.

A thin hand that feels listless in one's grasp denotes a weak constitution that has only sufficient energy to live. A cold, clammy hand can also be a sign of poor health, but is generally indicative of a sensitive and nervous person.

A person who keeps their hands closed while talking is distrustful in nature, has little self-reliance and can seldom be relied on by others.

When all the fingers (especially if the fingers are long) are seen always clinging, sticking, as it were, or folding over one another it denotes very doubtful qualities in the nature of their possessor and a tendency towards dishonesty.

Right vs. left hands

Generally speaking, the dominant hand is indicative of what the person has made of themselves, while the non-dominant hand shows the inborn tendencies. Therefore, both hands should be examined together to see if they are in accord. When they do, the traits indicated are all the more decided.

The dominant hand denotes the developed or active

brain, while the non-dominant hand shows the natural tendencies or inclinations. For someone who is right handed, when something is indicated on the left hand and not on the right hand, the tendency will be in their nature, but unless it also shows on the right hand it will never bear fruit or come to any result.

The markings of the hands, particularly of the dominant hand, change over time as the person grows and develops new skills, or stagnates in their development. The student of this subject must always keep this rule in mind and not be misled by some "marvelously good line" on the non-dominant hand, for such a mark will have no actual result unless it is also found on the dominant hand.

Even with people who claim to be completely ambidextrous, there will be one hand that predominates.

The seven types of hands

The seven types or shapes of hands are as follows:

(1) The Elementary--or manual labor type.
(2) The Square--or useful hand.
(3) The Spatulate--or nervous active type.
(4) The Philosophic--or jointed hand.
(5) The Conic--or artistic type.
(6) The Psychic--or idealistic hand.
(7) The Mixed hand.

The Elementary Hand

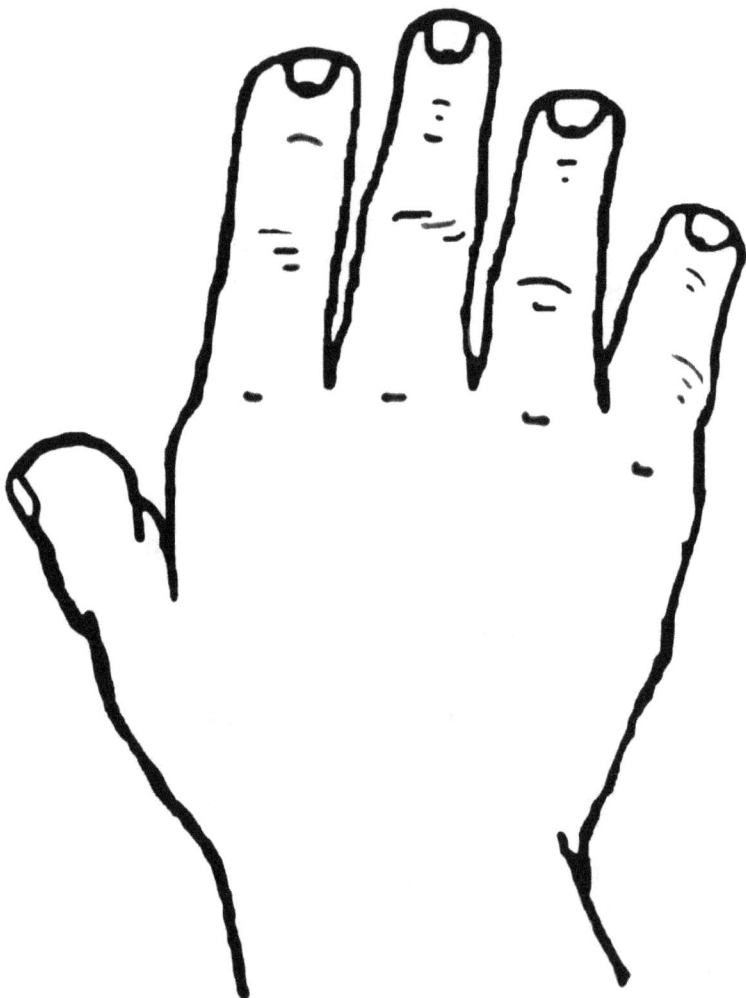

The elementary hand

The elementary hand is extremely short and thick set. The fingers are short and stubby. People having such hands are usually engaged in occupations requiring manual labor.

This hand has the least flattering portrayal of personality, indicating someone who is not very imaginative or intelligent, but before you make such a judgment about someone you should evaluate much more than simply your initial impression of the shape of the hand.

Note -- The thumb is extremely short and low-set with the elementary type.

The Square Hand

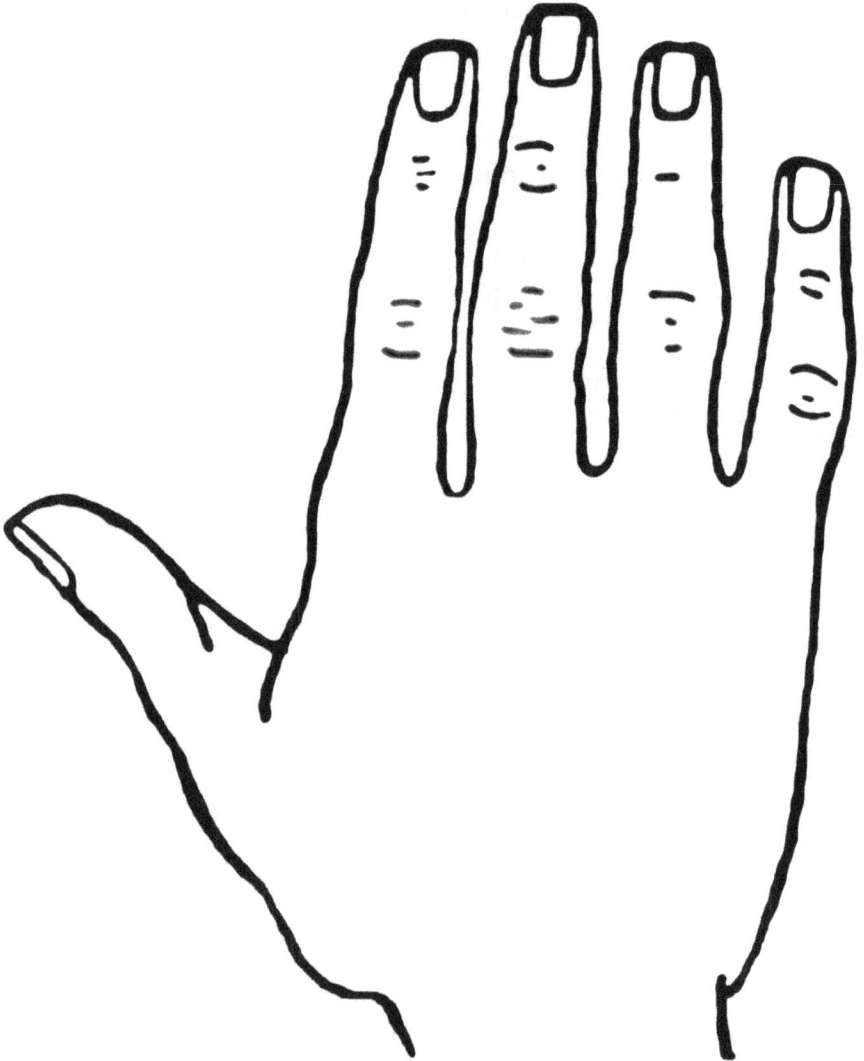

The square hand

The square hand is so designated on account of the palm being like a square in shape, or at least nearly so. It is rather straight or even at the wrist, at the base of the fingers, and also at the sides. The fingers themselves also have a square-cut appearance. The thumb is, however, nearly always long, well-shaped, and set high on the palm, and stands well out from the palm.

The square hand is also called the practical or useful hand. People who possess this type are essentially practical, logical, and rather materialistic. They belong to the earth and the things of the earth. They are solid, serious workers, methodical and painstaking in all they do. They believe in things only by proof and by their reason.

They can be determined or even obstinate, especially if their thumbs are long and the first joint stiff.

They succeed in all lines of work that do not require excessive amounts of creative imagination. As business men, lawyers, doctors, scientists, they do extremely well, and are generally to be found in such callings.

The Spatulate Hand

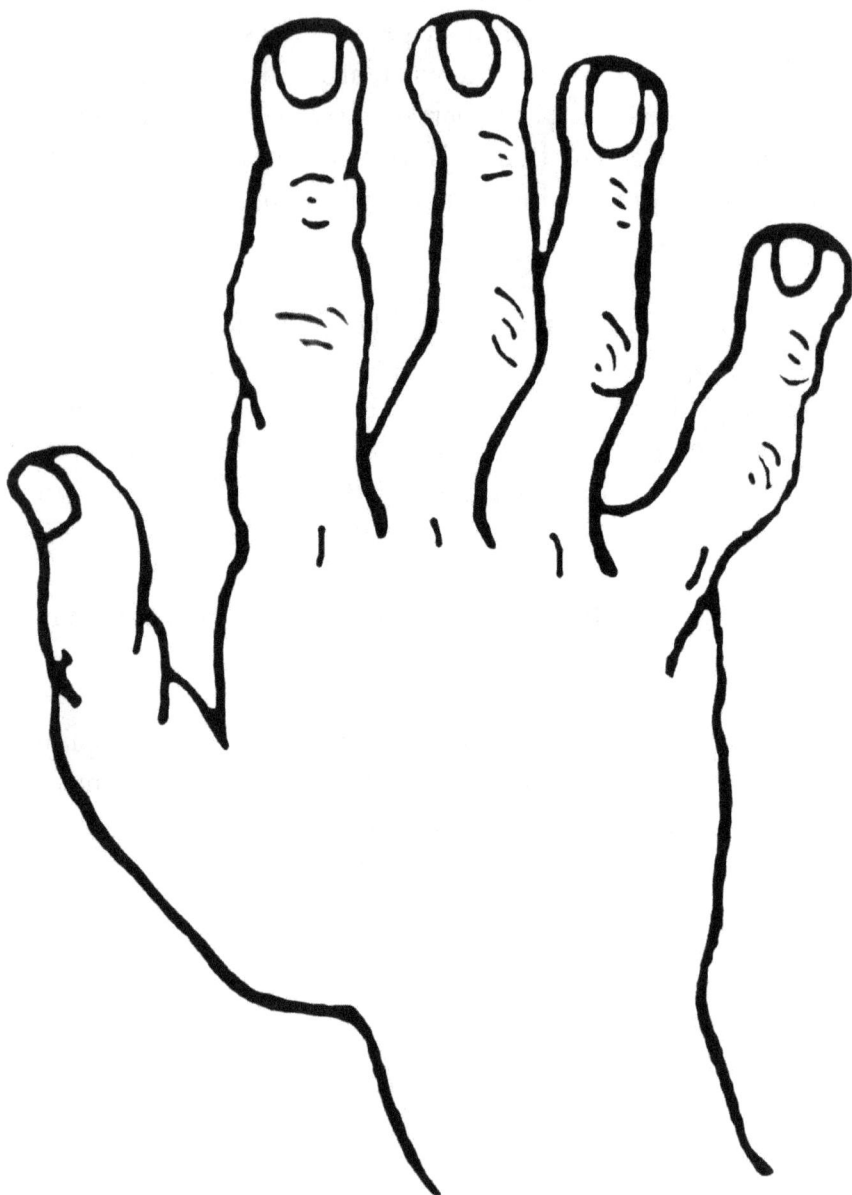

The spatulate hand

The spatulate or active nervous type hand is usually crooked or irregular looking, with large tips or pads at the ends of the fingers. The people who possess this type are in fact always pounding at something. They are full of energy, hard workers in everything they take up, and are generally remarkable for their originality.

They are not built on the hard-set square lines of the former type. These persons have enormous imagination with creative faculties largely developed. They are inventive, unconventional, emotional, demonstrative, and are the complete opposite in character to those who possesses the square type of hand.

The spatulate type has a palm that is irregular in shape. It may be wider at the base of the fingers than at the wrist, or it may be found vice versa. In the first case the person is more practical in their work and views, and less impulsive. With the larger development at the wrist, they are more carried away with their impulses, hasty and impetuous in temper, speech, and action.

The Philosphic Hand

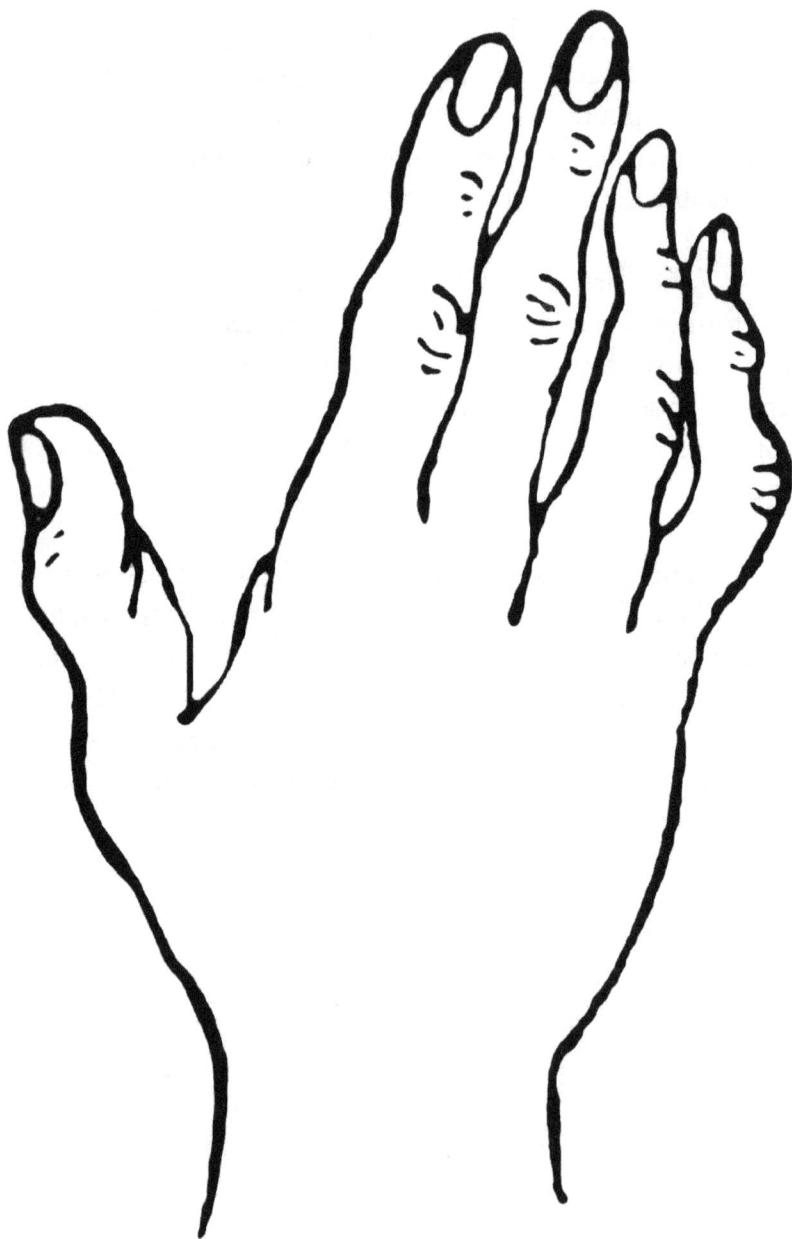

The philosophic hand

The philosophic hand received its name from the Greek word philos meaning love, and the Greek word sophich meaning wisdom. When the Greeks made a study of hands they noticed that all those persons who possessed this type of hand had a bent for philosophy in their blood that nothing could eradicate.

The philosophic hand is long, bony, and angular with knotty joints, and is as a general rule fairly thin. People with this type of hand are always studious. They are great readers and usually have a strong tendency towards literature. They love sedentary work, and have a somewhat lonely, ascetic disposition. On account of this quality they are very often found in church-life, or associated with religious movements. The monks of old who compiled those wonderful manuscripts on doctrine, science, art, alchemy, and occult matters all had this shape of hand.

It is more common nowadays to find a slight modification of the true philosophic hand where the palm is square, and with the fingers only belonging to the philosophic type. In such cases the practical nature is the basis or foundation on which the studious mind builds its theories in religion, literary achievements, or scientific research.

Generally speaking, people with the philosophic hand rarely accumulate as much wealth as those possessing the square hand.

The Conic Hand

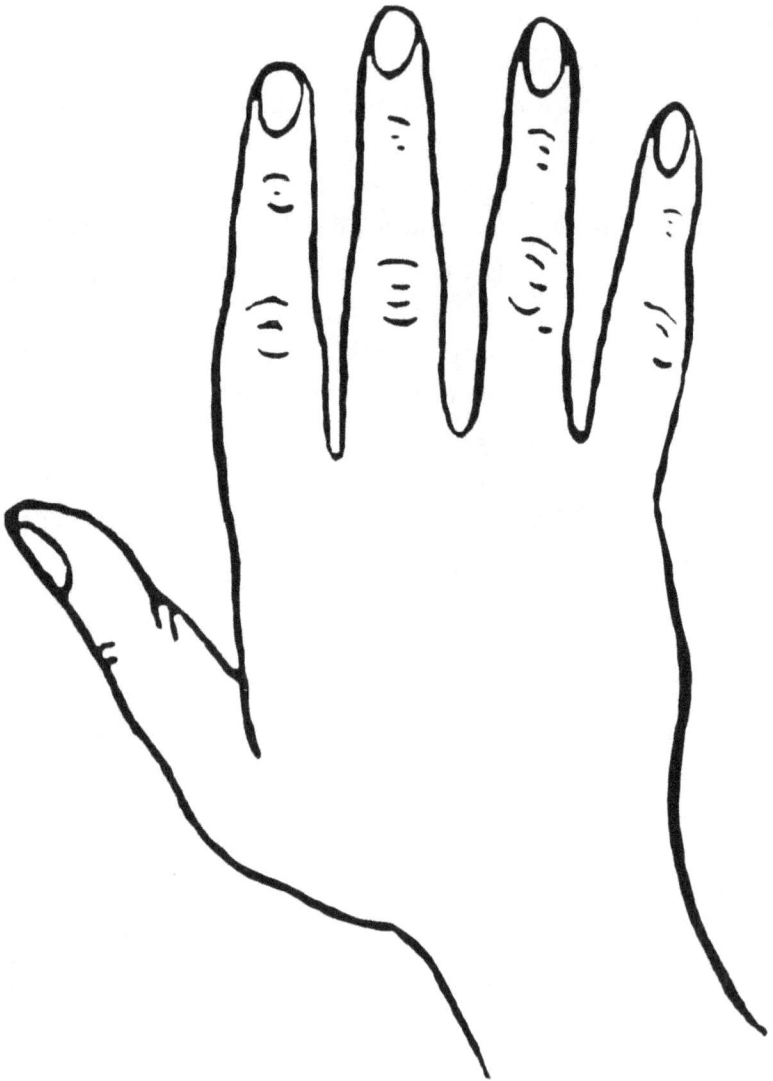

The conic hand

The conic hand is always graceful looking, with the fingers tapering and pointed. It has been called the artistic hand, not only on account of its appearance but also because of the qualities it represents.

Its possessor may not always paint pictures or design beautiful things, but will have the emotional, artistic temperament, which loves beautiful surroundings, and is most sensitive to color, music, and all the fine arts.

If the hand is full, fleshy, or soft, there is a laziness in their nature, which, if not overcome, combats the hard work necessary to achieve any real results. All very emotional people have more or less the characteristics of this type, but great numbers spend their time in the appreciation of art, rather than in making the effort to create it.

The harder and firmer this type of hand is, the more likely its possessor will make something out of their artistic temperament.

The Psychic Hand

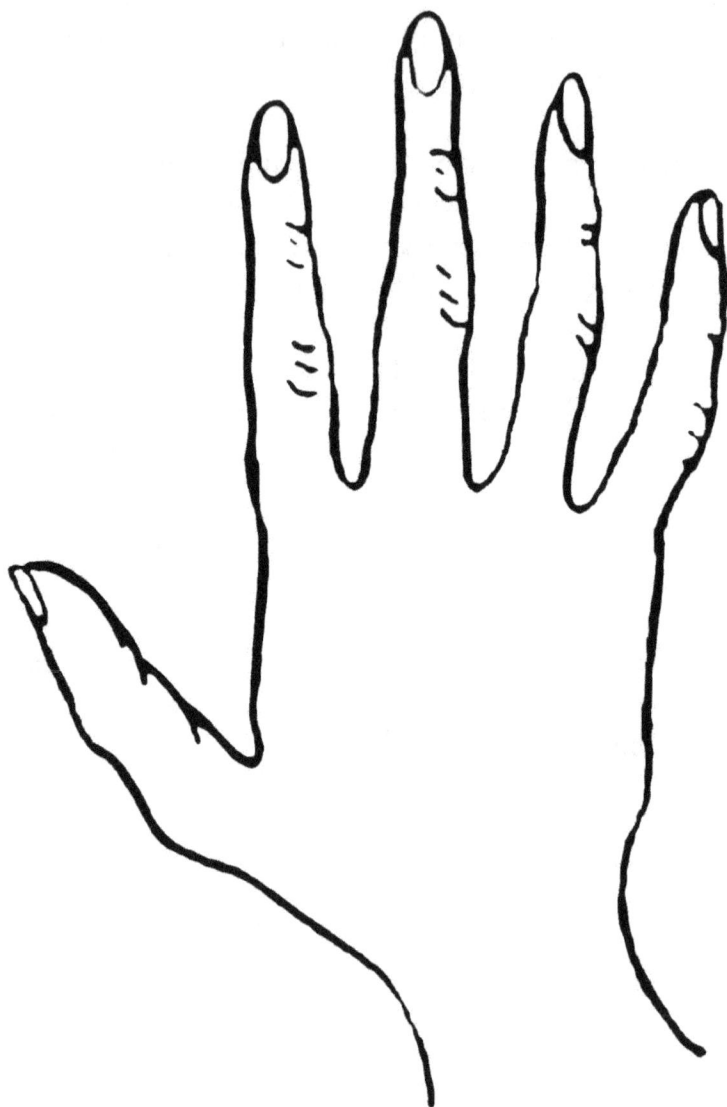

The psychic hand

The psychic or idealistic hand may in many ways be considered as the highest development of the hand on the purely mental plane, but from a worldly standpoint it is the least successful of all. Its possessors live in a world of dreams and ideals. They know little or nothing about the practical or purely material side of existence, and when they have to earn their own bread they gain so little that they usually starve.

These beautiful hands do not appear made for work in any sense. They are too spiritual and frail to hold their own in the battle of life. They are seldom strong physically, and consequently they are doubly unfitted for the struggle for existence. If they are supported by others, or have money of their own to live on, all may be well, and in such cases they will be likely to develop psychic gifts dealing with visions and ideals that few others would understand.

The mixed hand

The mixed hand is a combination of the types. Most hands are not purely one type; everyone has a combination of characteristics, but usually one shape is predominant. For a hand to be considered a mixed hand there must be several combinations present.

The mixed hand is often found to have all the fingers different from one another, as for example one pointed, one square, or spatulate, and so on. Or sometimes the palm may be of one type, say spatulate, with all the fingers mixed.

Such persons are always very versatile, but so changeable in purpose that they rarely succeed in making much out of any talents they may possess. They can generally do a little of everything, but do nothing well. They can talk on any subject that may crop up, but never impress their listeners with any depth of thought on a subject.

Conclusion

The hands are the immediate servants or instruments of the brain. There are more motive and sensory nerves from the brain to the hand than to any other portion of the body and, whether sleeping or waking, they continually and unconsciously reflect the thought and character of the mind or soul of the individual.

So, we can see from these observations that even without looking at the lines of the hand, one may be able to obtain certain details of character that are more indicative than those given by the face.

The Thumb

2

Character is shown by the thumb

The thumb is more expressive of character than any other part of the hand. There is a "thumb centre" in the brain and any pressure or disease in that part of the brain shows its effect in the thumb.

A large well-made thumb is the outward and visible sign of a strong-willed, determined person. The longer the thumb, the more the power of will rules the actions; the shorter the thumb, the more brute force and obstinacy sways the nature.

Love, logic, and will

The thumb represents love, logic, and will.

Love is represented by the base portion of the thumb, the part which is covered on the hand by the fleshy Mount of Venus. Logic is the middle phalange, and will is the top or nail portion.

When these divisions are large, the qualities are increased; when small, they play a smaller role in the life of the individual.

The nail phalange or will

The shorter and thicker the first joint or nail phalange is, giving the appearance of a club, the more ungovernable is the person in his or her temper. Such people have little self control and will fly into a blind rage at the slightest provocation. This curious formation has been called the "Murderer's Thumb" because so many who have committed murder in a mad fit of passion have been found to have this curious formation. The possessor of a clubbed thumb could not, however, plan out or premeditate a crime, for he would not have the determined will or power of reason to think it out. The shorter the thumb, the less self-control the individual has.

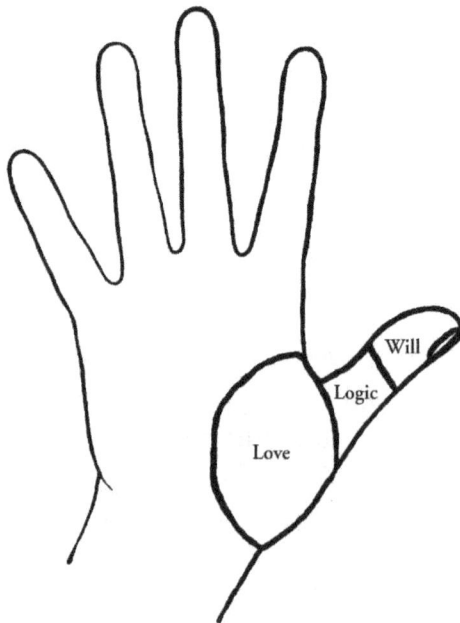

An employee with this type of thumb should never be given any position of authority over others, for they could not curb their ungovernable temper. A person with this type of thumb would also be absolutely unbalanced in their jealousy, and no one who has the ambition to live to the usual "threescore-years-and-ten" should risk marriage to a person with one of these thumbs. But as "love is blind" it is useless to give advice in such a case.

The nail phalange of the thumb, when long and thin, denotes the opposite of the above characteristics. In such cases the person has the most absolute control over their temper, their willpower is also strong but unobtrusive, and in a firm, determined way people with such a thumb manage others and bend those around them to their purpose.

The middle phalange or logic

The second joint, if delicately shaped, almost "waist like," indicates tact, diplomacy, and gentleness, also subtlety in argument.

If this part of the thumb is full looking, straight looking, or equal in size to that of the nail phalange, it denotes a person who cares nothing for tact and who, on all occasions, will speak his mind plainly, and with brutal frankness.

The "waist-like" thumb, and the "straight" formation, are the opposite of one another in their characteristics, but in this case the difference is in the quality of logic or reason. The former will not use or depend much on such things, he will rely, on the contrary, on tact and diplomacy to gain his point or win his way. The second group have little or no tact, but in all matters depend on argument and reason.

A tied-in thumb

When the thumb looks as if it were "tied in" close to the hand, the person is timid, easily frightened by both people and circumstances, narrow-minded in his views, and miserly in their habits. The thumbs of all misers are "tied in" and cramped-looking. It is perhaps this very fear of things and people that in the end makes them misers with their money. One need never waste one's time asking a person with one of these cramped-looking thumbs to do a favor.

The nearer the thumb approaches the side of the hand, or the more it looks tied down or cramped to the palm, the more the subject is inclined to grasp or hold. The true miser has always a thumb cramped towards the hand, and the nail phalange as a rule slightly turned in, as if the mind wanted to grab hold or retain.

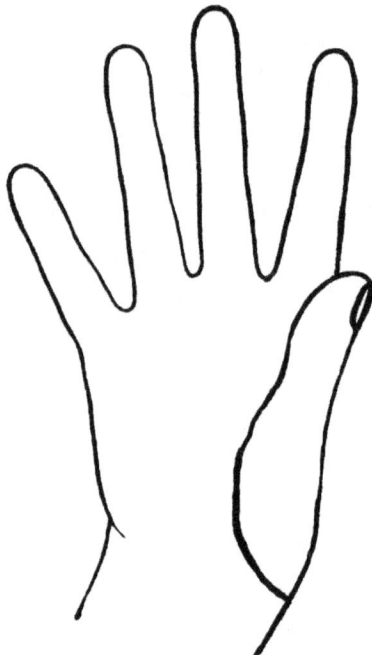

A right-angle thumb

A thumb standing very far out from the hand (almost at right angles to the palm) is not generally a good sign for success. Such people go to extremes in everything they do and are generally fanatics in religion, social reform, or whatever line of thought occupies their attention.

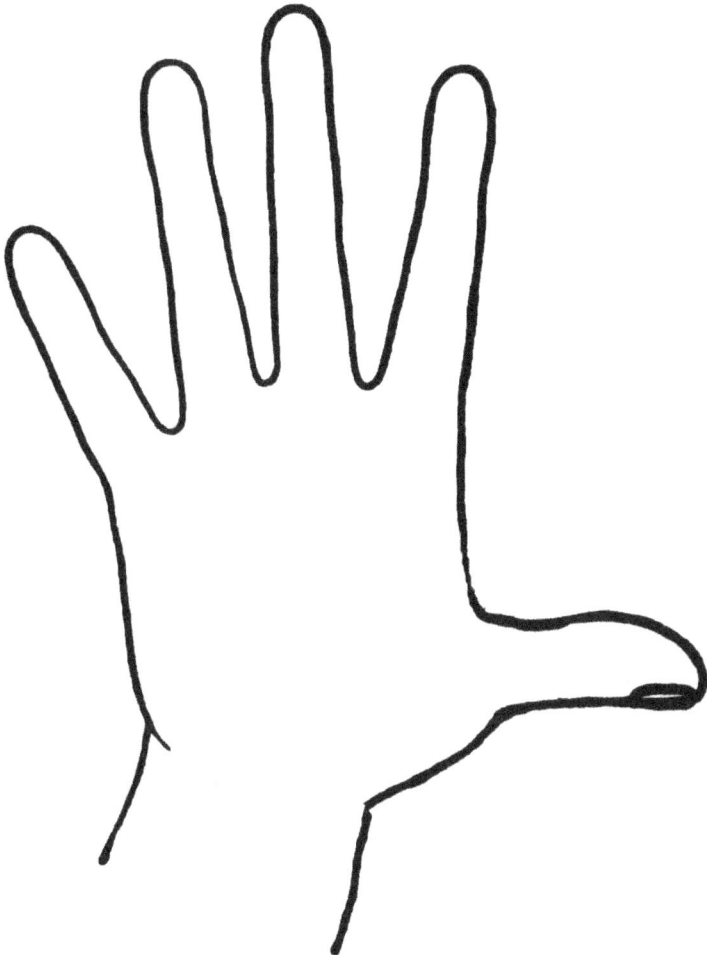

Firm-jointed Thumb

Supple-jointed vs. firm-jointed

There are two distinct classes of thumbs, the supple-jointed and the firm-jointed. The supple jointed thumb bends outwards at the joint underneath the nail. This denotes a nature pliable and adaptable to others, very broad-minded, rather unconventional, and not obstinate in its views of life.

These characteristics will be increased if the Head Line is sloping and bending downwards. If, however, the Line of Head lies straight across the palm, they are more conventional. The "supple-jointed" thumb also denotes generosity of both thought and money. In all ways these people are more extravagant than people who have the straight firm-jointed thumb. Possessors of such a thumb are generous, adaptable to others, extravagant, and impetuous in their actions and decisions. They promise things quickly and are more often heard to say "Yes" than "No"; but if they have time for reflection, they very often go back on their promises.

Supple-jointed Thumb

If a favor should be asked of the person with the supple-jointed thumb, one should remember that they are more inclined to give in on the impulse of the moment, and if one does not press one's point home at once, they are likely first to promise, and later, on reflection, change their mind.

Individuals having a "firm-jointed" thumb, on the contrary, cannot easily adapt themselves to others. They are distant and more reserved with strangers. The person with the stiff-jointed thumb is more likely to refuse at first and on reflection to agree to the proposition; but once they make up their mind, they will stick to their judgment or opinion, and the more they are opposed the more determined they will be to hold to their view. It is useless to oppose such people -- if one cannot lead them, it is no use attempting to force them against their will.

This type has more self-control than the type of people with the "supple jointed" formation, and is not so generous or extravagant. Individuals of this group, however, make more reliable friends, so their friendship, though difficult to obtain, is generally worth having.

The firm-jointed thumb is the outward sign of a more resisting nature, and the longer the first or nail phalange is, the stronger and more powerful the force of will.

These people seldom make friends so easily or rapidly as those belonging to the other type. They rarely begin a conversation with a fellow traveler.

The supple-jointed class, on the contrary, enter readily into conversation with strangers, and they often make their greatest friends while traveling. They are affable, charming companions, and give in readily to the wishes of others. In fact, this quality can lead to a weakness that should be guarded against. Among all those who take the "easiest way" a large majority will be found to have very supple-jointed thumbs. This, however, will be greatly qualified by the position and appearance of the Line of the Head, the indicator of the developed mental will.

To have a supple lower or middle joint does not relate to the will but to the logic of the possessor. When this second joint is found to be supple the subject adapts himself to circumstances rather than to persons. He reasons out that he must bend or adapt himself to the conditions or circumstances of the life in which he is placed.

The Fingers

3

A quick glance at a person's fingers can tell you a lot about the person.

Length of the fingers

If the fingers are long in proportion to the palm, they denote greater intellectuality and mental power. When short and stubby looking, the subject is less intellectually inclined and more physical.

If the fingers and the palm appear equal in length, the owner will tend to be practical and level headed.

If the fingers look unusually long and thin, out of proportion to the palm, the man or woman will err on the side of too much ideality and refinement and is not suited to business or work requiring "level headedness" and practicality. It would not be a good idea, for example, to put such a person in charge of employees. However, such a person would be suited for positions requiring more mental work, such as research, science, literature, or philosophy.

The fingers at rest

People whose fingers are straight and stiff even at rest tend to be methodical and have a stick-to-it quality. They are often considered stubborn and inflexible.

When the fingers are very supple in the joints and turn backwards or outwards from the palm the subject is "open-minded" and quick to grasp ideas or suggestions, but has a tendency to change their mind frequently. This is an indication of a quick wit and clever brain; but such persons lack continuity of purpose. They have no "hold," as it were, on any one thing.

When the fingers are curved inwards, the subject is cautious, and inclined to hold on to what they know or what they have. Such people have retentive memories and "hold" or grip, as it were, any one thing they may take up. They will not change their minds easily.

Spacing between the fingers

A wide space between the thumb and first finger denotes independence and fearlessness.

A wide space between the first and second fingers denotes independence of thought. These people are not easy to manipulate.

A wide space between the second and third fingers denotes independence of circumstances. Such as a person who is independently wealthy.

A wide space between the third and fourth fingers denotes independence of action. These people are not afraid to step out on their own. They often seem to march to the beat of their own drum.

The joints of the fingers

Persons with smooth-jointed fingers are more impulsive than those with "knotty joints". The "knotty joints" arrest the impetuousness of their disposition and give reflection and love of detail in all their work and are more frequently found in the hands of great organizers and those who require thought and reflection in carrying out their plans. The joints tend to become more pronounced as people age, reflecting the tendency to become less impulsive.

The fingers considered separately

Each finger indicates particular personality traits, but when a finger leans towards another one, it also takes on the qualities expressed by the finger towards which it leans.

The first finger is called the **Finger of Jupiter**. When it is long, it indicates a love of power and command over others. When short it denotes dislike of responsibility and lack of ambition.

The first finger is considered as the dictator, the lawgiver, the finger of ambition, the indicator, the pointer, etc. If this finger is unusually long and nearly equals the second, all these tendencies are extremely pronounced.

Therefore, if your employee has this finger long, you

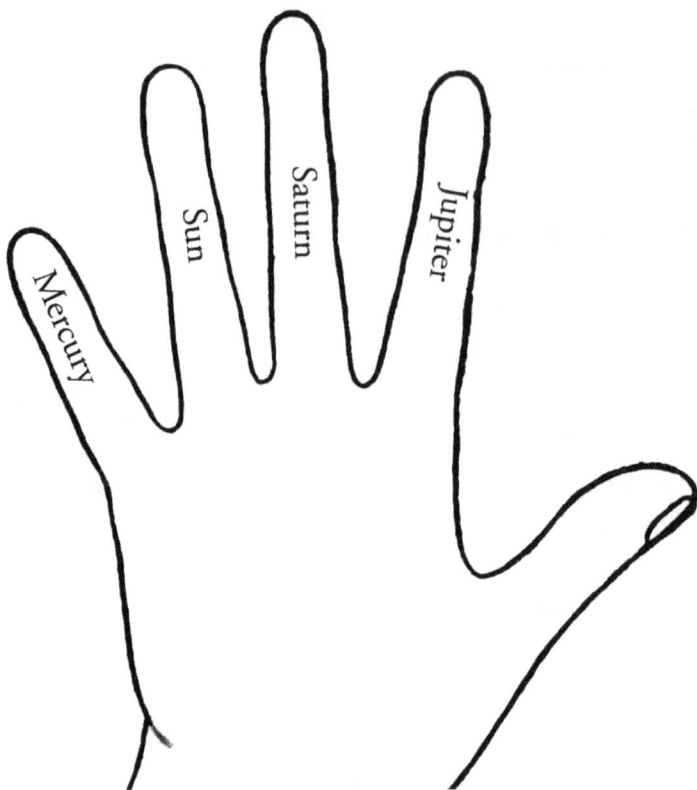

can safely entrust them with control over others. You will be amazed how well he or she will make rules and regulations and sees that they are obeyed; but beware, Mr. Employer, if your first finger is short in comparison to that of your employee, for, if such be the case, you too will have "to toe the line" and you may find yourself in a very disagreeable position.

But let me give you a further warning: Should this man or woman have a first finger that is long and crooked, you will assuredly find out to your detriment that the personal ambitions of such an individual are "crooked." Such an employee would be unscrupulous in finding out your secrets and getting you into their power.

The second finger is called the **Finger of Saturn**. When long it indicates prudence, love of solitude and a reserved, studious disposition. When short it denotes frivolity and general lack of seriousness in all things.

If the second finger is straight and well shaped, its owner will be very serious, a little inclined to melancholy, but will fulfill their responsibilities, but again beware if this finger is crooked. However, in this case the owner would be more subject to what may be called "a crooked fate" than willfully "wrong." Such people are, as a rule, the victims of strange circumstances over which they seem to have no control. They are continually getting themselves into trouble, but, more by a strange twist of fate rather than through their own willful actions.

The third finger is called the **Finger of the Sun**. When it is long it indicates love of the beautiful, desire for celebrity and fame, but when excessively long, the tendency inclines towards notoriety, risk in speculation, the love of money and gambling. When short it denotes a dislike of all these things.

The third finger, if extremely long and straight, indicates an extraordinary desire for glory, celebrity, publicity and the like; and although this might be an extremely good quality in the case of an actor, preacher, or politician, it may not be desirable for a private secretary, or the confidential clerk to some family lawyer.

If this finger is crooked as well as very long, all the above qualities will be intensified and exaggerated. The love of spending money and fondness for show will also be more marked, the gambling tendencies very pronounced. No position involving the handling of money should be entrusted to the possessor of such a finger.

The first and third fingers of equal length is the best sign of a balanced mind, but such a sign is rather rare to find.

The fourth finger, or little finger, is called the **Finger of Mercury**. When it is long (passing the nail joint of the third finger) it indicates mental power, grasp of languages, and power of expression, especially in speech and subtlety in choice of language. The saying "to twist a person round one's little finger" originated from this very sign. Such people have a marvelous gift of speech, eloquence and flow of language, valuable gifts, of course, for orators or persons in public office.

A short "little finger" denotes the reverse of the above. When short it denotes difficulty in speaking, and in the expression of thoughts. Such persons find the greatest difficulty in expressing what they want to say, but they can write better than they speak and should be encouraged to do so.

The shorter the "little finger", the more timid and sensitive these people are in the presence of strangers. If this finger is crooked, then these weaknesses are all the more emphasized, but if formed crooked and long, the power of eloquence is also crooked. Such people will tell any "fairy tale" to suit their purpose--they are natural born liars.

The nails of the hand

A study of the nails of the hand is a remarkably accurate guide to many diseases. They are peculiarly indicative of hereditary diseases, especially lungs, heart, nerves, and spine.

Warning: Never tell someone that their hands show a predisposition toward a particular illness, regardless of what you think you are observing, since the power of suggestion can actually result in their developing the suggested health problems. Unless you are a qualified medical doctor, never use the study of the hands in an attempt to diagnose illnesses in others. This information is strictly for use in studying your own hands.

The nails are divided into four very distinct classes; long, short, broad, and narrow.

Long nails

When the nail bed (the portion of the nail that is attached to the finger) is very long, the general constitution never appears to be as strong as when they are medium in size.

Persons with a long nail bed are more liable to diseases of the lungs and chest, even more so when these long nails are seen ribbed or fluted, with the ribs running upward from the base to the edge of the nail.

The same type of nail, but shorter in appearance,

indicates that the delicacy lies higher up towards the throat, and denotes a tendency for laryngitis, inflammation of the throat, and bronchial troubles.

When especially long nails are bluish in color, they denote a still more delicate constitution, coupled with poor circulation of the blood.

Long narrow nails

Very narrow nails indicate spinal weakness, and when extremely curved and very thin they indicate curvature of the spine and great delicacy of the constitution.

Short nails

A nail bed that is short in appearance denotes a tendency towards weak action of the heart, more especially so when the "moons" are very small or barely noticeable. When the nails appear very flat and sunk into the flesh at the base they denote nerve diseases.

When a deep furrow is found across the nail, it is a sign of recent illness and the date of this illness or strain can be very clearly determined. As it takes about six months for a nail to grow out from the base to the outer edge, the nail can easily be divided into sections. When the furrow or very deep "rib" is seen close to the edge, the illness took place about six months ago; when the furrow is seen about the centre, the illness was approximately three months previously, and when at the base, about one month previously.

White spots on the nails are a sign of general delicacy,

and when the nail is seen covered with small white flecks, the whole nervous system is in a low state of health.

The moons of the nails

Large "moons" denote strong action of the heart and rapid circulation of the blood, but when unusually large they indicate too much pressure on the heart, rapidity in its beat, and strain on the heart valves.

Small "moons" indicate the reverse of this; they denote poor circulation, and weak action of the heart.

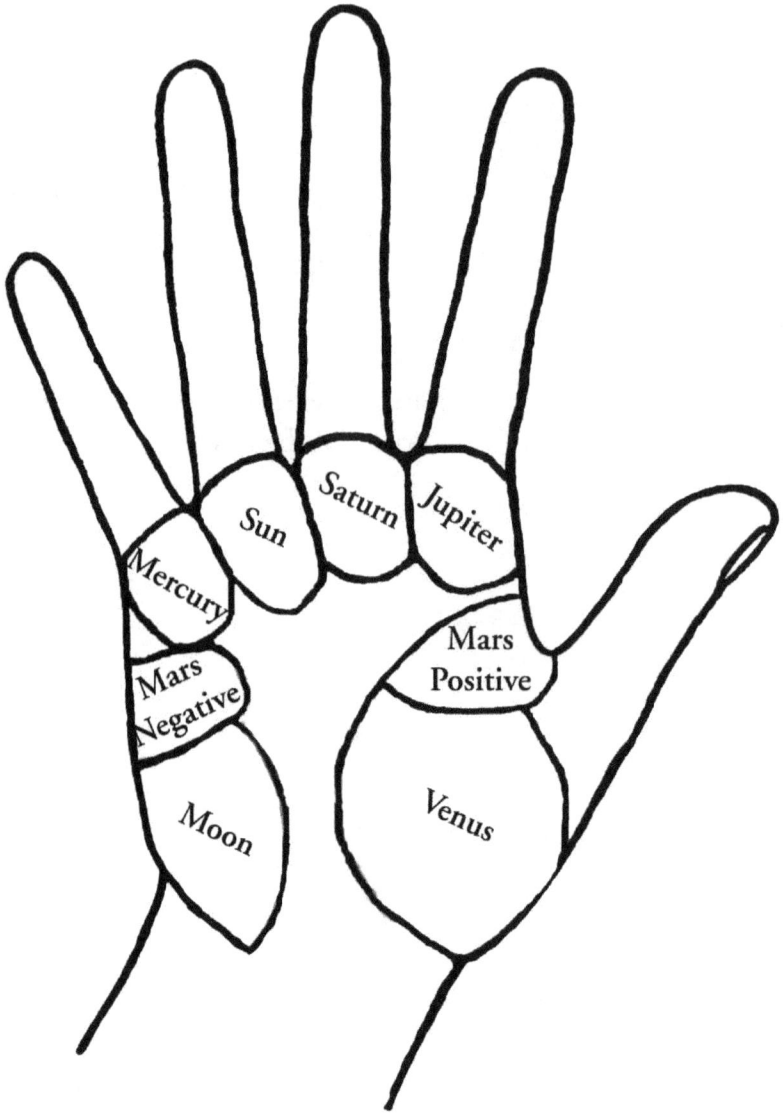

The Mounts of the Hand

4

The Mounts of the Hand

The mounts of the hand vary according to the character and dispositions of people's different temperaments.

In almost all southern and more emotional people, these mounts are more noticeable than those belonging to northern countries. I have observed that all people with the mounts apparent or prominent are more swayed by their feelings and emotions than those people who have flat palms and undeveloped mounts.

The names given to the mounts of the hand are those of the seven principal celestial bodies that influence the destiny of Earth: the Sun, Moon, Venus, Mercury, Mars, Jupiter, and Saturn.

These names were given to the mounts by the Greek students of this subject, and were associated with the following qualities:

Venus = Love, sensuality, passion
Mars = Vitality, courage, aggression
Mercury = Intelligence, commerce, science

Moon = Imagination, romance, changeability
Sun = Happiness, fruitfulness, success
Jupiter = Ambition, power, domination
Saturn = Reserve, melancholy, seriousness

A short explanation of Astrology

In my own long study of both astrology and palmistry I could not help but notice the intimate relationship between these two sciences. Although it is not within the scope of this book to teach Astrology, I must, point out the influence of the planets on our lives.

In the Zodiac there are what are called the twelve houses of the seven principal planets of our Solar System. The Zodiac itself is described both by astronomers and astrologers as a pathway in the universe, about sixteen degrees broad, in which the planets travel. It is divided into twelve signs or houses of thirty degrees each, and our Sun enters a new sign on an average of every thirty days. At the end of twelve months it has completed the zodiacal circle of 360 degrees, or one solar year.

The Sun, the creator of life, and itself the greatest mystery of our universe, is 330,000 times larger than our earth. It therefore follows that in entering a new sign of the Zodiac, it changes the magnetic vibrations of the effect of each sign towards our earth. Consequently it is reasonable to presume that a person born, say in April, and another in October, would have very different characteristics and naturally a distinct destiny, because of the position of the Sun at the time of their births.

To interpret the significance of the mounts of the hand first look at the hand and analyze which mounts are prominent. For additional insight consider the birth date of the individual and corresponding zodiac sign.

You will notice as you read the following chart that there are 14 possible aspects of the mounts but only 12 months or signs of the Zodiac. Those persons born between January 21 and February 18 have 3 possible influences.

Saturn Negative -- January 21 to February 18
Sun Negative - January 21 to February 18
Moon Negative - January 21 to February 18
Jupiter Negative - February 19 to March 20
Mars Positive - March 21 to April 20
Venus Positive - April 21 to May 20
Mercury Positive - May 21 to June 20
Moon Positive -June 21 to July 20
Sun Positive - July 21 to August 20
Mercury Negative - August 21 to September 20
Venus Negative - September 21 to October 20
Mars Negative - October 21 to November 20
Jupiter Positive - November 21 to December 20
Saturn Positive - December 21 to January 20

Keep in mind as you study the following that the word positive does not necessarily mean good and negative bad, rather it is more like positive and negative charges on a battery, neither good nor bad.

The Mount of Mars

This mount has two positions on the palm; the first is to be found immediately under the upper part of the Line of Life, and the other opposite to it in the space lying between the Line of Heart and the Line of Head. The first position relates to the physical characteristics and the second position to the mental characteristics. Usually only one or the other is large.

If the first position is large it is considered positive, and it has more importance when the person was born between the dates of March 21st and April 20th, and in a minor way until April 28th, which portion of the year in the Zodiac is called the House of Mars (Positive).

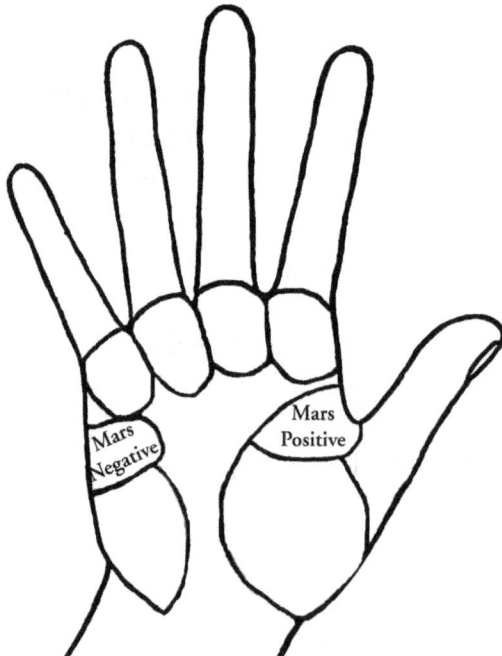

If the second position is large it is considered negative, and it has more importance when the person is born between October 21st and November 20th, and in a minor way until November 28th, because in the Zodiac this portion of the year is denoted as the House of Mars (Negative).

The Mount of Mars (Positive)

In the first Mount of Mars, at the beginning of the Line of Life, and especially when the subject is born in the House of Mars (March 21st to April 20th, and in a minor way until the 28th), the individual possesses a strong martial nature which will make its tendencies manifest in all actions of life, whether they be in business, a soldier, or a leader in any line whatever.

These subjects are born fighters in every sense of the word. They aspire to be leaders in whatever career they undertake, and with even average intelligence they generally become heads of business or organizations and take on large responsibilities.

They have great determination, they resent all criticism, they are decided and dogmatic in all their views, and seldom ask the advice of others, until it is too late to alter their purpose.

They must do everything their own way, and as they always believe their way is the only right one they resent the slightest interference from others, and will even turn on their best friend who may attempt to dissuade them from their plans or purpose.

They can only be handled or managed by kindness, patience, tact, or by their affections. The slightest attempt to fight or coerce them will bring them up "in arms" immediately. Their temper is hasty and explosive, but at the same time quickly over, and when the storm subsides they bitterly regret the outburst of passion and the cruel things they may have said in the heat of the moment.

As a rule these people are good-natured and generous, but erratic and impulsive in all their actions. Their greatest fault lies in their impulsiveness and lack of self-control, and unless a good Line of the Head is shown on the hands, they rush madly into all kinds of difficulties and dangers and often make a complete muddle of their opportunities and the magnificent powers of leadership that they nearly all possess.

These people as a rule are unhappy in their love affairs or domestic life. They rarely meet partners who understand them, and if they are lucky enough to escape opposition from their partners, they usually meet with it in their children.

Such people should be advised to cultivate self-control, and above all to avoid wines, spirits, and stimulants of all kinds, to which they are very much inclined.

They should endeavor to sleep more than others, to take more recreation and exercise in the open air, and above all things to curb their pride and control their temper.

Those among them who practice self-restraint can rise to almost any height in life and do great things for the benefit of their fellow men.

The Mount of Mars (Negative)

The second Mount of Mars, lying between the Heart and Head Line, if large is considered negative. This mount is more important when the subject was born between the dates of October 21st and November 20th and until November 28th. In the Zodiac this period of the year is called the House of Mars Negative or Mental.

In character they are very different from the former type, all the Mars qualities being in the mind and in the mental attitude towards people and things.

The latter type are mentally very courageous, and possess moral courage more than physical. They hate to have scenes, or to be mixed up with physical violence or bloodshed.

They love to fight mentally, however, and in debates or arguments they fight to the finish. They are more quietly determined than the former group of Mars subjects. They are even more obstinate in their views, but conceal their opinions, and often pass for assenting parties when in reality they are but waiting for the right opportunity to strike their "mental blow" and confuse their opponent.

These people make better organizers than leaders, and their mental martial spirit often finds a splendid field for their talents as the strategist behind an army. In plans, tactics and strategy, in carefully thought-out stores of ammunitions, provisions, or in financial schemes that may bring ruin on a more warlike enemy.

They can employ cunning and craft of every description to carry out their plans. They will stop at nothing to carry out their purpose, as such they can be the most treacherous and deadly enemies of all.

All these Mars Negative people have a mysterious power of magnetism which they seem almost unconsciously to use in their dealings with others. They make natural hypnotists and thought-readers, and have strong leanings towards occultism and secret societies of all kinds. They can use these wonderful qualities for the good of others, especially if they take up the study of medicine or science, for which work they are well suited.

Mars Negative people are generally so versatile and many-sided that they are the most difficult of all to place in some special career. If a good Line of the Head is found on the hand, then there is nothing in the world of mental endeavor in which they will not make a success. It is a curious fact that these people seldom carry out what they were first trained for, and in the course of their lives they are likely to change their profession or vocation as many times as the proverbial cat has lives.

The worst fault of this type of person is that they are rather too adaptable to their surroundings and to the people with whom they come in contact. If they are thrown with evil-minded persons they are inclined to adapt themselves to their companions and even attempt to "go one better," but if in contact with good influences they just as rapidly develop the best that is in them.

This period of the Zodiac has from time immemorial been symbolized by the figure of a scorpion stinging its own tail, and by an eagle with its head pointing upwards to the sky.

Such symbols perfectly illustrate the dual nature of this personality. In their lower aspect no type can be more vicious or harmful, even to wounding themselves and bringing about their own destruction. In their higher form, however, there is probably no group whose spiritual nature can, like the eagle, soar to such heights or be so free from earthly ties.

The Mount of Jupiter (Positive)

The Mount of Jupiter is found at the base of the first finger. When large, it shows desire to dominate, to rule and command others, to lead and organize, and to carry out some distinct plan. But these good qualities will only be employed if the Line of the Head is clear and long. When this line is poor and badly formed, then a large Mount of Jupiter gives pride, excess of vanity, an overly self-confident and self-opinionated person. However, there is no mount more excellent and no surer indication of success from sheer strength of character and purpose than a well formed Mount of Jupiter on an otherwise well marked hand.

This mount may be considered Positive when a person is found born between November 21st and December 20th, and in a minor way until the 28th. These persons are naturally ambitious, fearless and determined in all they undertake, but in acting on their impulses, they generally "hit too straight from the shoulder," or show their ambition too plainly, and so arouse antagonism, opposition, and enmity.

They concentrate all their attention on whatever they may be doing at the moment and see no way but their own, especially if they feel the least opposition to their plans. They are, however, honorable and high principled in almost all they undertake and respond to any trust or confidence placed in them.

They are usually extremely truthful and bitterly resent any attempt at deception, and do not hesitate to unmask any effort to deceive others, even when such an action on their part may ruin their own plans.

They have great enterprise in business and all matters requiring organization, and easily become the heads of businesses, or hold responsible positions in government offices or under the government. They rarely become politicians because they cannot bear to bend to any party plans or schemes.

They are perhaps the most independent of all types in choosing their own careers. Because their father may have happened to be a clergyman will be no reason for them to follow his example or even hold the same views on religion.

It is for this reason that in early life such subjects are a cause of worry and anxiety to their parents; but they should always be allowed to choose their own career and even change it a dozen times if they wish, until at last they find their true vocation.

Their great fault is that they are inclined to go to extremes in all things, and in doing so exhaust their efforts, and then change and fly off in another direction. But in all cases where the Line of Head is well-marked, especially when lying straight across the palm, there is no height in position or responsibility that they may not reach.

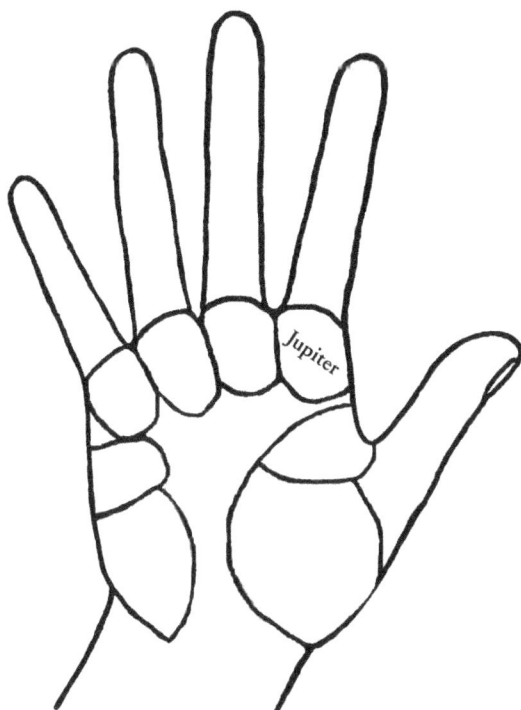

The Mount of Jupiter (Negative)

The Mount of Jupiter may be considered negative or mental when flat or underdeveloped, or when the subject was born between the dates of February 19th and March 20th, and in a slighter degree until March 28th.

In this case the ambition takes rather the mental form rather than what might be termed material. Mental work and mind development is more their specialty than other forms of effort.

They seem to possess a kind of natural understanding of things and easily acquire all sorts of knowledge about a large variety of things, especially the history of countries, races, peoples, geographical, botanical, and geological research.

In spite of this mental ambition, these people are usually so very sensitive and so lacking in self-confidence that they find the greatest difficulty in carrying out their plans and making people believe in their projects. For this reason they appear to shrink from coming before the public, and have to stand aside and see others getting the credit for what really was their plan.

A great number of literary people, composers and artists are born in this period and exhibit all the qualities that it represents. It is again a strong clear Line of the Head which, if found on the hand, will determine whether the mental will power is sufficient to make this type overcome its natural sensitiveness and use the great qualities they have to carry out their aims and ambitions.

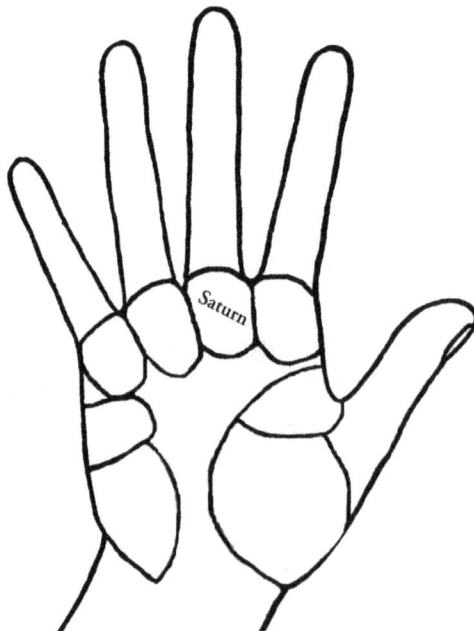

The Mount of Saturn

The Mount of Saturn is found at the base of the second finger. Its chief characteristics are love of solitude, prudence, quiet determination, the study of serious somber things, the belief in fatalism and in the ultimate destiny of all things.

A complete absence of this mount indicates a more or less frivolous way of looking at life, while an exaggeration of it denotes an exaggeration of all the qualities it represents.

The Mount of Saturn (Positive)

The Mount of Saturn may be considered positive when large and well developed, or when the subject was born between the following dates, December 21st and January 20th, and during the subsequent seven days while this period is fading out and being overlapped by the period following.

People born in these dates have strong willpower and intelligence, but they usually feel exceptionally lonely and isolated going through life.

They are very much children of fate and circumstances, over which they appear to have no control.

In character they are usually remarkable for their independence of thought and action, and they detest being under the restraint of others.

For kindness and sympathy they will do almost anything, but they usually feel so isolated that they scarcely believe in the affections that may be offered.

They have strange ideas of love and duty, and for this reason they are usually called somewhat peculiar by those few who attempt to penetrate their isolation.

They have a deeply devotional nature, even when appearing not to be religious, and they make every effort to do good, especially to the masses, even when there may be no likelihood of their getting recognition or reward for their efforts.

Such people as a rule feel the responsibilities of life too heavily and in consequence often become despondent and gloomy or retire into their own shell.

If at all inclined to be religious, they generally go to extremes and become fanatical in any church they may adopt. Mysticism and occultism of all kinds appeal very strongly to their inner nature, but here again they are also inclined to go to extremes.

They admire clever, intellectual people, and are deep thinkers in all matters that interest them, but they cannot tolerate interference in their views from others.

They are often found holding positions of great responsibility, but in all matters fatalism seems to play a strange role in their life. They seem chosen to be the instrument or mouthpiece of destiny, often hurling thousands to destruction in what they believe is their duty. If called upon to make a sacrifice of their own flesh and kin they will be the first to plunge the knife into the heart of their dearest.

The Mount of Saturn (Negative)

The Mount of Saturn may be considered negative or mental when small and underdeveloped, or when the person was born between the dates of January 21st and February 18th, and also for the seven days following.

These people are like the preceding type in almost all things, except that the same things appear to affect them more mentally than physically.

They also feel lonely in life, but more mentally than the former type--they seem to feel less companionship in their ideas and thoughts, whereas the former feel it more in their lives and careers.

These latter types are more sensitive and very easily wounded in their feelings. They read character instinctively and seem to "see through" people too easily to be really happy. They bitterly resent being taken in or deceived, and when they think they have been, they astonish people by the bitterness of their resentment.

They make loyal, true friends, if their feelings are once aroused, and they will undergo any sacrifice for the sake of a friend, but they will stop at nothing to avenge an injury if they think they have been deceived.

They are usually very active for the public good, and they give a good deal of their time and money to doing good, but in their own way. Like the positive type of Saturn they have very decided views of their own about religion and especially the regular observances and ceremonies of church life.

They are very different from the previous type in that they usually take a keen interest in public meetings and large gatherings of people. They love theatres, concerts, and places of amusement, and yet they feel alone in life.

They have a quiet controlling power with their eyes, and although highly nervous people themselves, they have the greatest control over excitable and nervous patients and also over the mentally disturbed. It is a strange fact that during their careers they seem destined to be brought into contact with such cases.

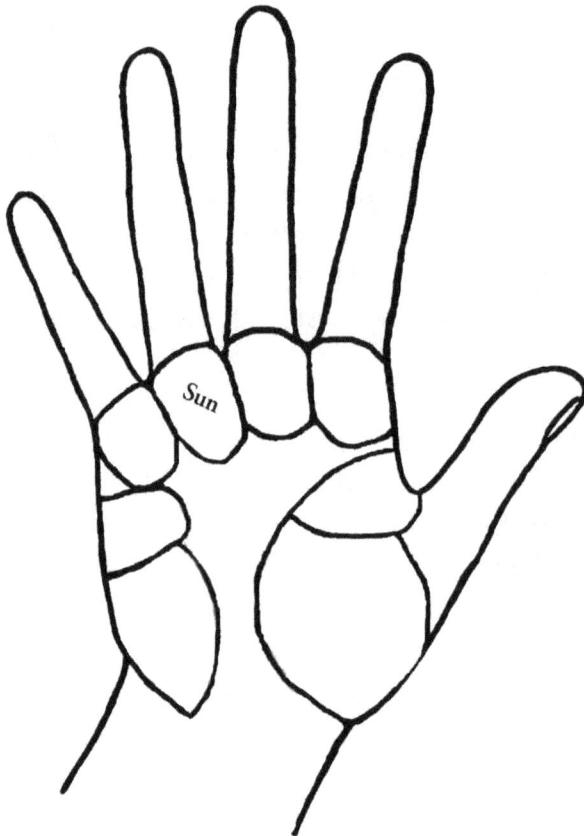

The Mount of the Sun

The Mount of the Sun is found under the base of the third finger. To this mount the Greeks also gave the name of Mount of Apollo.

When large or well developed it indicates glory, publicity, a desire to shine before one's fellows. It is always considered a good mount to have large.

It also indicates enthusiasm for the beautiful in all things, whether one follows an artistic calling or not. People with this mount large, even if they have success in practical life, build beautiful houses or have artistic surroundings of some sort. They also have an expansive temperament, are generous and luxurious in all their tastes. They are bright and sunny by nature and have a forceful, happy, lucky personality.

The Mount of the Sun (Positive)

This mount may be considered positive when large and well developed, or when the subject was born between the dates of July 21st and August 20th, and generally until the 28th of this month, which portion of the Zodiac is called the "House of the Sun."

These people represent what may be called the heart force of the human race, and as a rule are generous and sympathetic even to an extreme.

They have great force of character and personality, and even when constrained by circumstances to exist in the lower walks of life, they play, even there, a role distinct from their fellows, and their clean-cut, well-marked personality is sure to make itself apparent.

At heart they are really most sympathetic, though they often seem to hide this quality. They have no mercy for "weaklings" or evaders of the truth, and in brutal frankness they will even denounce their own children should they find them falling into evil ways.

They display the greatest loyalty if any friend of theirs is attacked, especially if in an underhanded way. They love intensely and they hate intensely. Theirs is no middle path, for they must be either at one extreme or the other.

Although truthful and naturally honest they often get terribly deceived, and the danger for such people is that towards the sunset of their lives, the glorious Sun that has shone through them gets darkened by the deceit and treachery of others.

Many of these people who have cheered others, who have brought their grand sunshine of good into the hearts of others, cannot cheer themselves when the twilight comes, and so they often fall victims to gloom and melancholy.

Among their other characteristics these people are extremely proud and would sooner die than ask favors from others. They are extremely easily wounded through their pride and are unusually sensitive.

Impetuous and hot-tempered, they make many enemies, and when engaged in public life, which they are usually well fitted for, they often find themselves bitterly attacked in the most unscrupulous manner.

The Mount of the Sun (Negative)

This mount may be considered negative when small or underdeveloped, or when the subject was born between January 21st and February 18th, and for the seven days following.

In this case they are far more successful when managing for others than for themselves.

They are usually found most active in their plans towards the relief of all distress and for what they believe to be the public good.

They are also often found in governmental positions, or as leaders of some party or section of public opinion. Usually they take the part of the "underdog," and cause themselves to be greatly abused and disliked by the richer and more powerful classes.

They seldom attract wealth as do those of the Positive type, who are usually lucky in money, and when they do they are inclined to impoverish themselves in their efforts to help those around them, or in the execution of their philanthropic plans for the good of the poorer classes.

In strange apparent contradiction to this, these people are usually excellent in business and in their financial plans, but again it is more for others than for themselves. Many of them make fortunes for others and keep the merest pittance for their own homes.

As a rule, they find great pleasure in public ceremonies,

and meetings of all kinds. They love theatres and all places where large numbers of people congregate, and when wound up to the occasion they can display great eloquence, power of argument, and influence in debates. They rarely hold the positions they win for the run of their careers, they seem to play the role of the moment, and when that is passed they just as quickly retire into obscurity or into a quiet private life, and often end their days in the most unusual or unheard-of places.

Quite the reverse of the Positive type, these people can endure any kind of martyrdom or suffering. They are buoyed up with the feeling they have done their duty to their fellow beings, and this feeling seems to sustain them against all disappointments, or losses or attacks on their name.

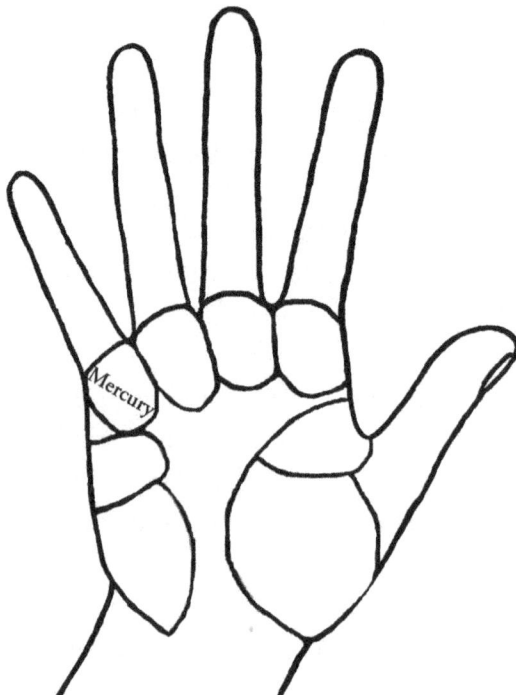

The Mount of Mercury

The Mount of Mercury is found under the base of the fourth finger. On a good hand it is a favorable mount to have, but on a hand showing evil tendencies, especially mental, it increases the bad indications.

It seems to relate more to the mind than anything else. It gives quickness of wit, thought, and eloquence. It also relates to adaptability in science and commerce, but if evilly afflicted, it denotes mental excitability, nervousness, lack of concentration, trickiness in business, and everything that is unreliable in character.

This mount should always be considered with the kind of Line of the Head found on the hand. With a Line of Head long and well marked, it increases all the promise of mental aptitude and success, but with a weak, badly marked, or irregular Head Line, it augments all its weak or bad indications.

The Mount of Mercury (Positive)

This Mount can be considered positive when large or well developed, or if the subject was born between the dates of May 21st and June 20th, and until the 27th of that month, but during the last seven days its influence is considered dying out and not so strong.

People born in this period are represented in the Zodiac by the symbolism of the twins. It is a curious fact that all persons born in this part of the year are singularly dual in character and temperament. One side of their nature may, in fact, be described as perpetually pulling against the other, and although nearly always possessed with unusual intelligence, they often spoil their lives by lack of continuity in their plans and in their purpose.

They seldom seem to have a fixed idea of what they really want. They change their plans or their occupations at a moment's notice, and unless they chance to be very happily married, they are just as uncertain in marriage.

They are the most difficult of all classes to understand. In temperament they are hot and cold in the same moment, they may love passionately with one side of their nature and just as quickly dislike with the other.

They are very critical, and especially notice small faults or mannerisms in others, and they can express their views with a sarcasm that is as cutting as it is clever.

In all business dealings or affairs where a subtle, keen mind is useful, they can out-distance all rivals, provided they are sufficiently interested to enter into the competition.

They are excellent in diplomacy and are gifted talkers, but they usually leave their listeners at the end of their conversation no wiser than they were at the beginning.

They are the most delightful people imaginable, but one must never expect them to be the same today as they were yesterday.

They believe that they are the most truthful persons in the world, and so they may be at the moment they are telling the story, but to them moments seem entire lives, and so in a day or a week the same story may have a totally different coloring. It is unlikely that these people will admit this to be true of their character, but a little study will convince anyone that it is a fairly accurate description of this subject's chief characteristics.

Mental work, especially the class of mental work that requires quickness of wit and change, appeals to them more than any other. They make clever actors, barristers, public speakers, diplomats, stock brokers, company promoters, or inventors of new methods in business. In all careers that require keenness of mind, they can attain success, provided they have developed a sufficient amount of will power and continuity of purpose to stick long enough to any one thing.

The Mount of Mercury (Negative)

This mount may be considered negative when flat or underdeveloped, or if the person was born between August 21st and September 20th, and until the 27th, but these last seven days of this period are not so marked, but take more from the characteristics of the incoming sign.

People belonging to this negative type of the Mount of Mercury have all the good points of the positive class, and even some added in their favor. For example, they stick longer and with more continuity to whatever study or career they adopt. They have hardly the quickness or the brilliancy of the first type, but they have a more solid, plodding course of action, and as a general rule they make more out of their lives.

They are also more materialistic and practical in their views of life, but they analyze and reason everything from their own way of thinking outwards towards others. If they see a thing is right, it is right to them, and for this reason they are often found doing exactly the opposite from what one would expect.

Women born in this period are especially curious puzzles. They are either extremely virtuous or the direct opposite, either extremely truthful and conventional or the reverse; but whether good or bad, they are all a law unto themselves, and in all things they usually think of themselves first.

Women born in this period often abandon their husbands or their children just because they think they ought to do so. They also are liable to change their religious views half way through life, or from the most conventional suddenly become the reverse. In the same way women who have commenced their career by leading unconventional lives, may just as suddenly become religious and enter some extremely severe order or community.

Again, as in the positive type, it is the Line of the Head that must be carefully considered if one attempts to predict what they will eventually become. If it is clear and straight, their best qualities will, as a rule, come to their rescue; but if weak or poorly marked, it is more than likely that the evil side of the nature will in the end predominate.

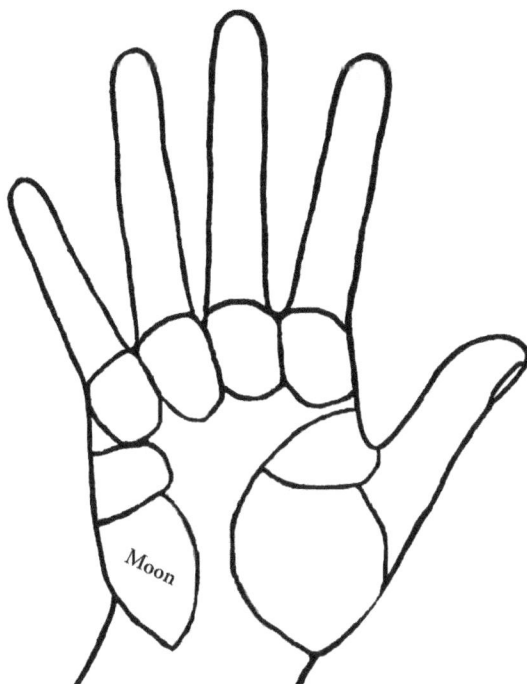

The Mount of the Moon

The Mount of the Moon, or as it is also called the Mount of Luna, is found on the base of the hand under the end of the Line of the Head.

This Mount relates to everything that has to do with the imaginative faculties, the emotional artistic temperament, romance, idealism, poetry, change of scenery, travel, etc.

The Mount of the Moon (Positive)

This mount may be considered positive when it looks high or well-developed, and also when the subject is found to be born between the dates of June 21st and July 20th, and until July 27th.

People who belong to this group are gifted with strong imagination which colors everything they do or say. They are intensely romantic, but idealistic in their desires, and have not that passionate or sensual nature that is given by the Mount of Venus on the opposite side of the palm.

As a rule they have well developed creative faculties, and succeed with inventions and in all new ideas in whatever careers they undertake. Even business people born in this period are remarkable for their originality, and the inventive manner in which they will tackle the most practical affair. They are, however, inclined to speculate or even gamble in stocks, business or, in fact, anything in which they are engaged.

Although their imagination is large, they often achieve great success and make money in business. Some great financiers and heads of large organizations have been born in this period and have also had the Mount of Luna very highly developed on their hands.

It has been said that what one sees in one's dreams one shall gain in reality, as a result, imaginative people have been found among the most successful of all classes. Imagination may be another name for inspiration.

People born in this period are seldom bound by any rule of thumb or set convention. They love what is new in everything, and perhaps for this reason they love travel and change, and generally see the greater part of this planet before they voyage over the last river of all.

Change in every way affects their careers as it does

their lives. Even the successful members of this period have more ups and downs than almost any other group. They rarely, however, give in to the blows of fate. Their imagination probably helps them through, and they seldom remain down or down-hearted for long.

Inventors, artists, musicians, and composers are found among people of this type, but almost without exception they have a love of mystic and occult things, and their dreams and visions are tangible and clear.

These children of the Moon are even more magnetic and successful when the Moon appears in the heavens. Even their health appears to change and become better under her benign influence, and they should always be advised to commence their plans or operations when the Moon is to be seen illuminating the skies.

That the Moon plays an important role in the affairs of this earth cannot for a moment be doubted. There are other thinkers besides those interested in occult subjects who have noticed the effect of the Moon on mundane things. If the Moon can affect vegetables, eggs, and the growth of chickens, as it has been proved to do, how much more easily and wonderfully it must affect the grey matter of the human brain, which is the most subtle and mysterious essence of all.

People born in this period should be most careful of those with whom they associate, because they are extraordinarily sensitive to the magnetism of others.

They should, if possible, avoid marrying early in life unless they are absolutely sure they have met their affinity.

These natures both change and develop rapidly, and they have a strong tendency to "grow away" from those with whom they associate in early life. It is the same with partners in business; they should be as much as possible "on their own" or, if partnerships are made, they should not be of a binding or restricting order, and provision should always be made for the partnership to be dissolved when it has become irksome.

The Mount of the Moon (Negative)

This mount is considered negative when it appears very flat on the hand, and it may also be taken as negative when people are found to be born between the dates of January 21st and February 18th, and in a minor degree, until about February 25th.

People born between these dates have good mental powers, but their imaginative faculties are seldom as much in evidence as is so strongly the case with the positive period.

These persons, on the contrary, are good and quiet reasoners-out of problems and matters relating to the organization of business, and are also excellent in all forms of government work. They make splendid heads of departments and rise to any responsibility very quickly and easily.

They are high-minded and have very decided views on love, duty, and social life. They make great efforts to do good to others, but as a rule their best work is done towards helping the masses more than individuals.

They are extremely kind-hearted and love to give a helping hand when they can, but at the same time they have an unfortunate knack of making many bitter enemies, and when holding government positions they are most bitterly attacked by the opposition press. Their work seldom receives its proper recognition and reward until they have passed from their sphere of influence, or have left this world of mistrust and ingratitude.

They generally make excellent speakers, but more from "plain speaking," in a particular way of their own.

As a rule they espouse the unpopular cause and take the part of the underdog in a fight.

They make devoted and loyal friends once their friendship is aroused, but at the same time they are extremely sensitive and easily wounded by those they care for.

They are strongly inclined to be religious and generally bring their religious views into all they do. They are in danger of becoming too fanatical, and when opposed, they become extremely obstinate, dogmatic, and hard to manage.

Heavy responsibility for others suits them best of all, especially if such responsibility lies in the form of government work, or in some position of management.

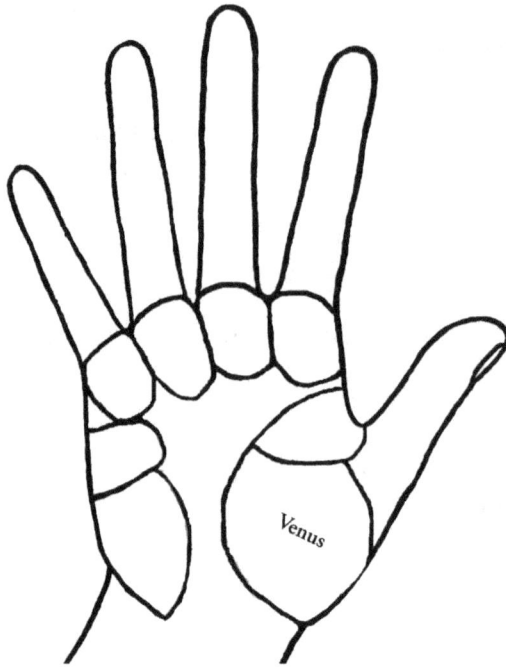

The Mount of Venus

The portion of the palm under the base of the thumb and inside the Line of Life is called the Mount of Venus.

When well-formed and not too large, it denotes a desire for love and companionship, the desire to please, worship of beauty in every form, the artistic and emotional temperament, and it is usually very prominent in the hands of all artists, singers, and musicians.

This mount covers one of the most important blood vessels in the palm the "Great Palmer Arch." If this loop or arch is large, it indicates a plentiful supply of blood and strong active circulation; consequently, the health is more robust. It is found that persons possessing this mount well developed, being in active strong health, are naturally more full of passion than those individuals in poor health, and who, in consequence, have this portion of the hand either flat or poorly developed. Hence, when this mount is large it shows passion and greater sensuality than when it is flat, flabby, or non-developed.

This mount is called positive when high or large, and negative when small or flat.

With the rest of the hand normal, this mount well shaped is an excellent sign to have, as it denotes magnetism and attraction of one sex to the other, but if found together with vicious or abnormal signs in the hand, it increases those tendencies.

The Mount of Venus (Positive)

The student may consider it positive when the subject is born between April 21st and May 20th, and in a minor way until May 27th, the chief characteristics of this period being that these persons have a curious dominating power over others, and are found rather inclined to be too dogmatic in their opinions, and also often too unyielding and tyrannical. They are considered stiff-necked and obstinate, but the strange thing is that when they love they become the most abject slaves of all to the object of their devotion, and they will consider no sacrifice too great for that one being who holds or attracts their affection.

They are hospitable and generous, and especially love to entertain their friends. They make wonderfully good hosts, have great taste about food, and love to give excellent dinners.

They dress with great taste, and are generally considered richer than they really are, and they can make a good show on very little.

They are impulsive in their likes and dislikes, rather too frank and outspoken, quick in temper, and when their blood is up they have no restraint on what they say. Their passion or temper is, however, quickly over, and when the storm is passed they are most regretful for the wounds their temper may have caused.

These types are most easily influenced by their surroundings, and become morbid and depressed when they are forced to live in gloomy and uncongenial conditions.

People born in this period should not marry early, for their first attempt is usually a mistake. They are so independent in character that, especially if they marry early and find their mistake, they lead unconventional lives and get severely criticized in consequence.

They are inclined to be very jealous when their affections are roused, especially if the peace of the home is in any way disturbed.

The Mount of Venus (Negative)

This mount may be considered negative when the subject is born between the dates of September 21st and October 20th, and in a minor way until October 27th, and with people born in this period it is seldom found so prominent. The fact is, that the affections these subjects possess may be just as intense, but more mental than physical.

Their love is spiritual rather than sensual, and they crave more for soul companionship than for that of the physical senses.

Of course there are exceptions to all rules, but these exceptions can be easily seen by watching if the Mount of Venus is large with people born in this period.

All mental characteristics rule very strongly. Those born in this period have keen intuition and a mental balance not given to the other group. They have presentiments and psychic experiences, dreams, clairvoyance, and such like, which they often spoil by their reasoning faculties, and they endeavor to answer all problems through the medium of their mind or mental faculties.

In love they are nearly always unhappy. They cannot "let themselves go," like the Positive Venus type. They hesitate and miss their opportunities while they think or reason, and so love goes by and often leaves them nothing but regret. They should be advised to act more on their first impressions and intuition, and take the opportunities that fate throws in their way.

They occupy themselves very much with all mental questions concerning their fellow beings. They are often found studying law, but more with the desire of improving it for others than for their own personal advantage.

They have a great desire for knowledge, and often spend their lives in studying obscure subjects, but always weighing and balancing each point in the most conscientious manner. They make excellent doctors, judges, lawyers, but more as masters of some particular branch than that of gaining worldly advantage.

The Line of the Head

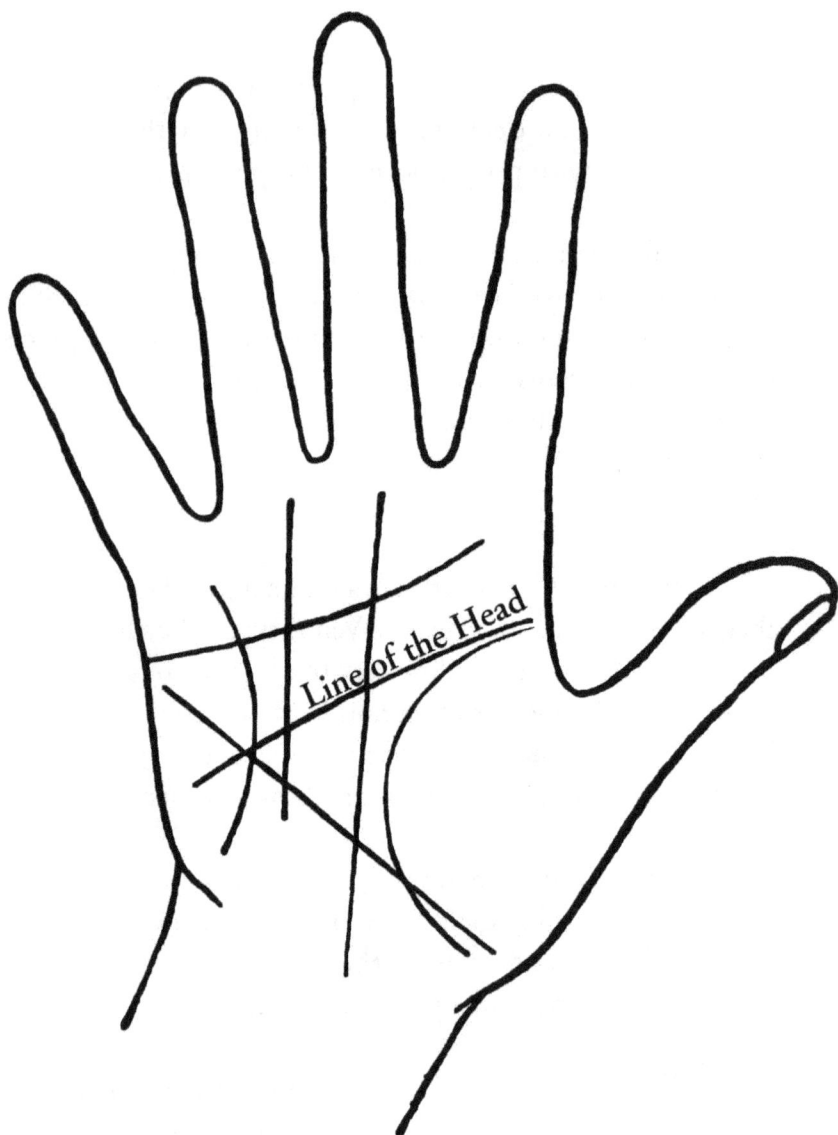

Line of the Head

5

The Line of the Head

The brain is always growing and changing

I regard the Line of the Head or the Line of Mentality as the most important line to study on the hand.

The Line of the Head is like the needle in the compass, without a true knowledge of which it is impossible to grasp the "direction of the subject." I have seen more mistakes caused by a lack of grasp of this point than by anything else. Many students make the mistake of paying great attention to what looked like a good Line of the Sun or Success, and, at the same time, not noticing a weak, badly formed Line of the Head, which contradicted the promise of success given by the various lines. If, on the other hand, the student had first noticed the Line of the Head, he would have seen that the promise of success was not backed up by the intelligence or the mentality.

As regards the future being foreshadowed, it has been demonstrated that the brain is always growing, changing, increasing, or diminishing. These changes commence years before the effect is shown by the thoughts or actions of the individual. A boy ten years old may at that point commence a development which will not be felt until he is thirty, and then it may change his whole life and career. As this development commences at ten, even at that age it has affected certain nerves, and they in their turn have already affected the Line of Head--a full twenty years before the point of change or action has been reached. It therefore follows that the future may be seen and told by a careful examination of the hand which, as Aristotle has said, is the "organ of all organs, the active agent of the passive powers of the entire system."

The Line of the Head and its variations

The two hands must be carefully compared--the left showing the inherited tendencies, the right the developed or cultivated qualities. The slightest change or deviation in the markings from the left to the right should be carefully noted.

The direction or the termination or end of the line should, be distinctly noted, for the all-important reason that this shows the direction that the mind is inclined to develop towards. For example, if found with the end of the line sloping downwards in the left hand, and having become straight or lying across the palm in the right--the student is safe in concluding that the subject has not been able to follow his natural bent, but by the force of circumstances has been obliged to make himself more practical, to study business methods, and to have undertaken a training towards practicality and level-headedness in order to rise equal to the circumstances that he found himself forced to meet.

In this way the student obtains an insight into the earlier conditions of the life under examination that is invaluable, especially when there is, as will be found in many cases, no Line of Destiny visible in the early years.

Mental qualities inherited from the parents

If, on the contrary, the Line of the Head is found exactly in the same position on the right hand as on the left, or even very nearly so, the student can be sure that there was little or no strain in the early years, but that the subject had easy conditions which were favorable, and which allowed him to develop his natural bent of mind.

If, however, it is found that the left hand shows a forked ending to the Line of the Head, namely, one end sloping downwards and the other end straight, or nearly so, and that the right hand shows only the straight line, then the student may decide that the subject inherited from the parents two natures, the imaginative and the practical, and that they chose to develop the latter, either in the direction of business or science.

In such a case, the student may state with confidence that the parents of the subject were decidedly opposite in their characteristics. If the line has become straight in the right hand the subject takes more after the side that was practical.

Boys or men tend to take more after their mother's mental peculiarities, and girls or women take more generally take after the mental qualities of the father.

On a man's left hand that has the forked ending with the upper end straight, or nearly so, the student can state that the mother was the more practical of the parents. If

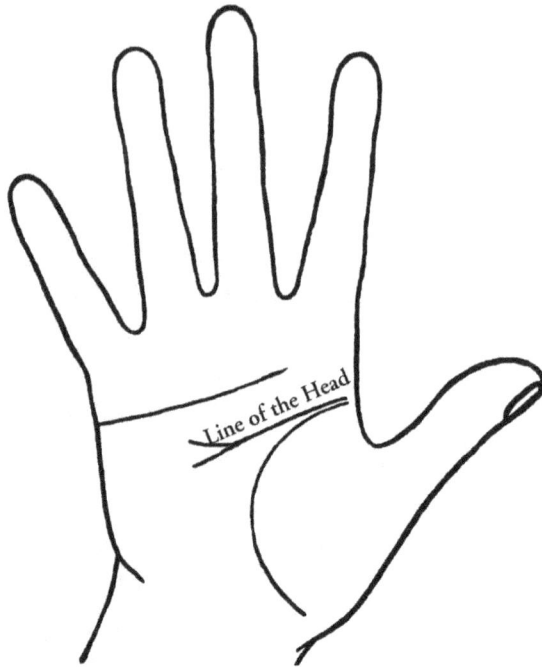

Line of the Head

on the right hand the same mark has become clearest, the man developed, followed, or cultivated the mental qualities of the mother more than those of the father. When reading a woman's hand the reverse will apply.

If, on the contrary, the lower line was more developed on the right hand, then the subject, if a man, had developed the imaginative or artistic qualities of the mother, and vice versa if the subject be a girl or a woman.

When the Line of the Head looks light or faint on the left, and strong and clear on the right, the student can safely state that the subject did not inherit any strong mental bent from either parent, but has cultivated and developed his own mind.

In such a case the subject has studied diligently, and

has become mentally superior to his or her parents. This is often found in the case of "self-made" men or women, who have had little or no education in their early life or in their home, but who from an innate love of learning developed themselves mentally. Such a sign would speak volumes for the willpower and ambition of the subject under examination.

If the Line of the Head is lighter and poorer on the right hand than on the left, the student can state that the subject has not made the most of his opportunities mentally, and that he has not, and never will, equaled the brain power and education of his or her parents.

In such a case one may also be sure that the subject has less willpower, although he might be very obstinate by nature, which will be seen from the quality exhibited by the nail phalange of the thumb.

The quality of the line

A poor or non-developed Line of the Head in the right hand is also the indication of a lack of purpose or ambition-there being no ambition where a lack of mental desire and development is so distinctly shown.

A clean cut deep Line of the Head is a more powerful sign of mentality than when the line is very broad, or lying, as it were, merely on the surface of the palm.

A wide broad line shows less concentration and a more vacillating changeable nature. This rule applies with equal truth to all the lines on the palm.

Broad, coarse-looking lines are more a constitutional sign than a mental indication. They are often found in cases where the subject leads a robust outdoor life, and those who have developed the physical side of their nature more than the mental.

Great mind workers usually have thin, fine, clean-looking lines, and especially that of the Line of the Head.

By observation the student will be able to class the sort of life led by the person under examination. No matter how intellectual a man or woman may look, the lines on the hand will indicate whether or not they have developed their mind. In this way, a study of the hand becomes a far more accurate guide than the study of the face. Many men and women may have intellectual faces and yet prefer sport or outdoor life to any mental pursuit or exercise.

The beginning of the Line of the Head

Turning from an examination of the direction of ending of the Line of the Head, the student must next examine the indications of the beginnings of this important Line. For example, the Line of Head may commence in three distinct different ways.

(1) From inside the Line of Life
(2) Joined to the Line of Life
(3) Outside the Line of Life

From inside the Line of Life

The first is the most uncertain of all. It denotes an over-sensitive, over-cautious, timid person. It also indicates a highly nervous, easily excited individual, one who has little control over himself or his temper, who is easily put out over trifles, and liable to do the most erratic things, or fly off at a tangent when irritated. Such people are always in trouble, generally fighting or quarrelling with those about them and over things that are of no consequence. They are likewise so easily wounded in their feelings, that even a look or an imagined slight will upset them for days.

If this Line of the Head farther out in the palm becomes straight, it denotes that the subject will, later, by the development of his intelligence largely overcome this failing of over-sensitiveness. If the line slopes much or bends down

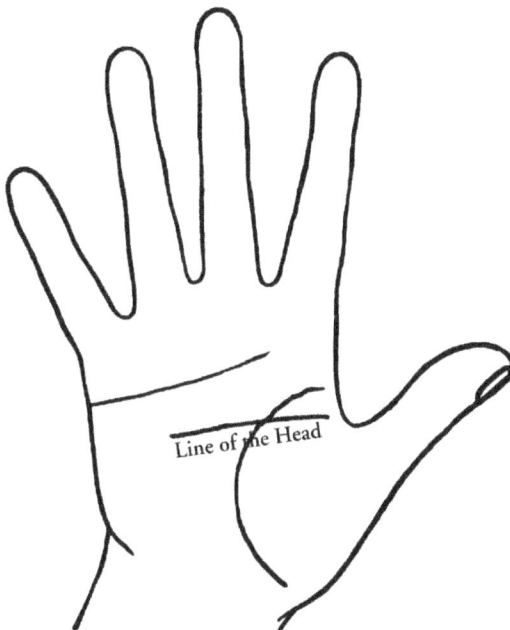

Line of the Head

towards the wrist or on to the Mount of Luna (the Mount of Imagination), then the subject will become still worse with his advancing years. If the Line of the Head is also poorly marked, or with "hairlines" from it, it is often an indication of some form of mental instability which is likely to cause the subject to be placed under restraint in later life.

If, with this latter indication, the student also finds all the upward main lines, such as the Line of Destiny, fading out past the middle of the palm, the indication of mental instability becomes all the more certain.

This type of Head Line is largely found in cases where the subject is naturally inclined towards drink and overindulgence of every description.

Even in cases where there are good lines running up the palm, it will usually be found that the subject gives way to the occasional desire for drugs or alcohol. The qualities of the fiery Mount of Mars, from which such a Line of the Head starts inside the Life Line, is largely the cause of these peculiarities. The opposite Mount of Mars on the side of the hand, on the contrary, gives mental control, so that even when the Line of the Head runs out straight on the palm it partakes of this "Mental Mars" quality, and so denotes that later on in years the subject with such a Line of the Head will be able to develop mental control. The sloping Line of the Head, however, would denote that the subject allows himself to turn, as it were, away from mental control, and so lets the earlier tendencies become his master.

This point alone is worthy of the consideration of all parents, and if observed by them would do much to help such children to develop mental control.

The Line of the Head joined to the Line of Life

The position of this line indicates in all cases a highly sensitive disposition, which is inclined towards caution and also lacks self-confidence. Even the cleverest people with this sign seem to rein themselves in too tightly, and are always inclined to undervalue their capabilities and talents.

When, with the same indication, the line is also sloping slightly downwards, the sensitiveness is still more increased. This form is largely found on the hands of artists, painters, and those who even in other walks of life have the sensitive artistic temperament, even though it may not have been developed to a larger extent.

If, on the contrary, the Line of the Head joined to the Line of Life runs straight out across the hand towards the mental Mount of Mars (Mars negative), the subject, though still extremely sensitive, has got greater courage of his opinions.

Such people do not get credit for being as highly sensitive as do the other people with the line sloping downwards towards the Mount of the Moon. The straighter the Head Line, the more the subject can be more relied on to carry out his determination, and often these highly sensitive and even nervous people are found doing very determined work in connection with some battle for principle or for right which they believe is their moral duty to carry out.

If this type of Line of the Head, however, goes very far across the hand and straight on to the mental Mount of Mars, it indicates an extremely strong-willed determined person who has the power to hide his sensitiveness and nervousness and stake everything for what he believes his duty to carry out.

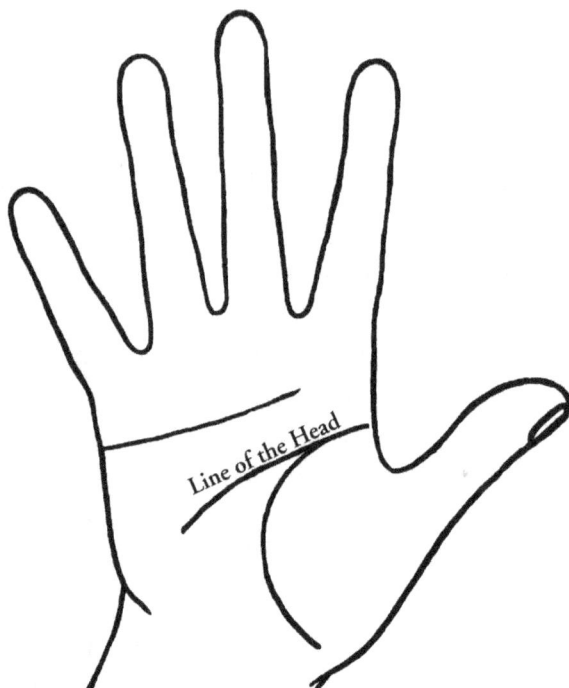

Line of the Head

The difference in the observation of these two distinct classes of individuals, namely, those with the Line of the Head joined but sloping, and the Line of the Head joined and straight across the hand, has caused many exponents of this study to make great mistakes in the judgment of their subject. When, as is very often the case, the Line of the Head is forked, also when joined and when these forked lines are equal to one another, especially in cases where the Line of the Head is joined to the Line of Life showing the sensitive temperament, this forked mark often indicates a certain degree of indecisiveness. The subject is inclined to balance too much between the two qualities of the mind, the practical and the imaginative. As to what they should do for the best, in such cases it is always wise to advise the subject to act according to first impulse either in dealing with practical or imaginative things. By so doing they employ intuition, and by using it do not waver and vacillate by too much reasoning over the question or endeavoring to see both sides of it at once.

When the sloping Line of the Head has a gentle curve downwards towards the Mount of the Moon, distinct control over the imagination is indicated. The student will then know that the subject simply uses his imagination when he wishes to do so instead of being controlled by it.

But the contrary is the case when the line bends too far down this mount. In this case the subject is the slave of his imagination and generally does erratic and peculiar things or can only work in moods of the moment. People of this latter class seldom, if ever, produce the great results in the world of art or imagination as do those who have the line simply curving downwards into this Mount.

When the Line of the Head bends completely down and turns with a curve under the base of the Mount of Luna, there is a tendency toward morbid imaginings and extreme sensitiveness, that people on whose hands it is found generally separate themselves from the rest of their fellows, and retire from the world altogether and live a solitary life. Their extreme sensitiveness makes life for them almost unbearable. In all such cases, there is extreme imagination, extreme sensibility, and a tendency to melancholy.

The Line of the Head separated from the Line of Life

The Line of the Head is more frequently found connected with rather than separated from the Line of Life. When the space is not very wide, it is an excellent mark to have, giving independence of thought, quickness of judgment, and a certain mental daring that is invaluable in fighting the battle of life. When the Line of the Head is at the same time lying fairly straight across the palm, such individuals have an immense power over others, but their capabilities are always more distinctly shown if they should in any form go in for some kind of public life.

People possessing this mark are less diligent students than those with the Line of the Head and Line of Life joined together, but they have such brilliancy and quickness of thought that they seem to see in a flash that which takes the other class hard work to attain. But these people with the open Line of the Head must, above all things, have purpose in their life. Without purpose they are like a ship drifting on an idle sea. They may spend their life in an aimless way unless the tide of ambition turns their way and carries them onward.

The same class of line but sloping is the more uncertain of the two characters, because the person is still more inclined to work only by moods. If the mood or the desire does not come, such people, although always brilliant and clever, may often waste their lives doing nothing.

Those people with the Line of the Head open and ascending slightly upwards towards or on to the mental Mount of Mars, are self-appointed leaders, organizers of any public movement. They will sacrifice everything, home, affection, and all ties for what they believe is their public duty in connection with the work that they have undertaken.

The Line of the Head very open and separate from the Line of Life denotes a character with too little caution or sensitiveness. The subject will go to the opposite extreme of those with the Line of the Head and Line of Life joined. When the space is very wide it denotes excessive impetuosity and lack of continuity of purpose, a person who pushes himself forward on all occasions, a great desire for notoriety and one continually changing his plans as far as the world is concerned.

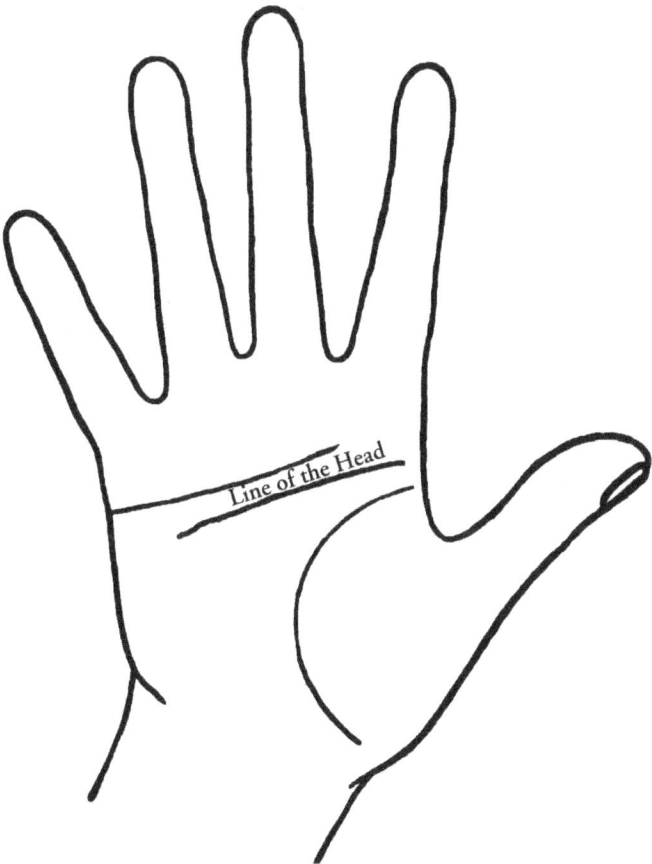

Line of the Head

When this line is excessively open or separate from the Line of Life, the brain seems to be an extremely excitable one. The subject suffers greatly from excessive blood to the head, mental hysteria, sleeplessness, and all things that affect the brain. If the Line of the Head is badly formed with islands, or a broad line with breaks and hair lines, it is just as much a mark of mental instability as the Line of the Head curving downwards at the wrist. A Line of the Head with islands indicates a character that will be more likely to be excitable and fly into a violent temper.

A Line of the Head not too widely separated and either with one end of it commencing on the Mount of Jupiter, or with its main branch from the Mount of Jupiter, is one of the most brilliant marks of all. The student must carefully establish this difference in the position of the Line of the Head in his own mind, as well as the termination or the ending points of this line. Determining these two points is the key to understanding the subject's character.

The Line of the Head and its secondary signs

What are known as "islands" in the Line of the Head are very important, especially if they are considered both in relation to the age at which they occur (see chapter on timing), and also in relation to the state of mind itself.

The principal rule the student must bear in mind is, that islands must be considered as showing a weakness in any line wherever they may be found, and are to be considered unfortunate signs.

On the Line of the Head when found in the form of

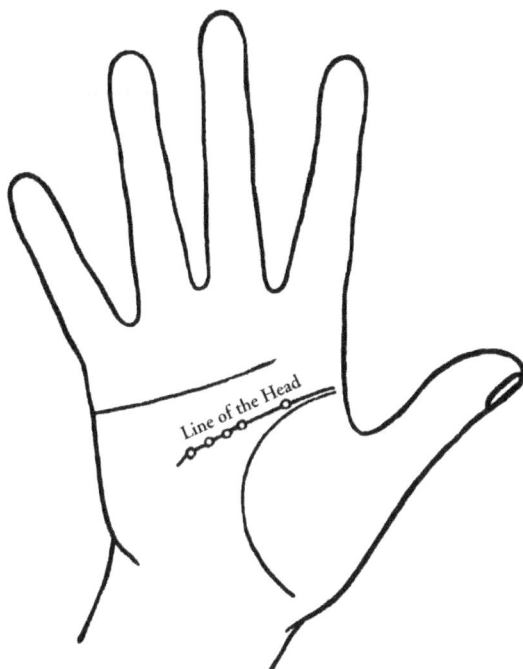

Line of the Head

a continuous chain, all through the line, they denote mental weakness, but generally produced by ill-health which more immediately affects the brain.

Such mental weakness or "brain illness," if found with nails showing very small "moons" or none at all, denotes an anemic condition of the blood that affects the brain, a low condition of vitality and bad circulation, which seems to starve the brain of blood and prevents such people from making any continuous effort in regard to study or willpower, and causes them to act in an erratic fashion.

If at the same time the Line of the Head is seen placed very high on the hand, this sign is worse still in its meaning, and such subjects are inclined to be mentally unstable at times.

When the Line of the Head is widely separated from the Line of Life, then this chain formation of islands is still more accentuated. Such subjects have periods of mental excitability which it seems impossible for them to control, and in such moments they are liable to commit mad or rash acts, dangerous to other people.

When, however, the Line of the Head is sharply sloping, with this formation of islands the subject is inclined to suffer from depression, during which he is likely to shrink away from people.

In relation to the islands in the Line of the Head, it is important to note their position on the line itself, or under what finger they make their appearance. When these islands are found at the beginning of the line under the first finger or Mount of Jupiter, it will be found that the subject in early life displayed no desire to study, was listless and without ambition.

Under the second finger on the Mount of Saturn, the subject, on the contrary, is inclined to suffer from severe headaches, morbidness, and melancholy. If the line looks weak or frays into little hair lines from this point out, it shows that the subject will never recover thoroughly from this malady.

Under the third finger, the Mount of Sun, an island shows a very curious fact, namely that the person is inclined to suffer from weakness of the eyes and short-sightedness. If many of these islands are marked it generally foreshadows a still greater tendency to blindness and weakness of the sight.

Islands under the fourth finger, the Mount of Mercury, and the extremity of the Head Line denote weakness of the brain in old age, and a highly nervous worrying disposition. If very badly marked they denote that in the latter part of life the subject may be disposed to mental instability proceeding from a worrying disposition, and often from the overstraining of the mental faculties. It will thus be seen that every portion of this remarkable line may be divided into sections to obtain marvelous detail in making predictions for the future. This line can further be divided, showing with considerable clearness the ages at which troubles or changes in the mentality may be expected (see chapter on timing).

Timing according to the Line of the Head

Under the first finger the period of the life indicated is the first 21 years, the second period contains another section of the three 7's, and lasts until 42 years of age; the third period of 7's which will be found under the third finger indicates the section from 42 to 63, and the fourth section which takes in the remainder of the hand, under the fourth finger, stands for the period from 63 up to the end.

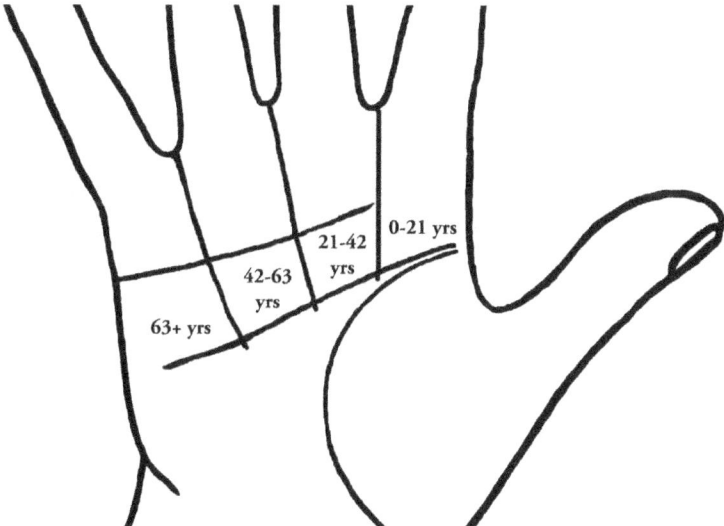

Changes in the Line of the Head

Another extremely interesting point in studying the Line of the Head is to take notice of certain changes in its position, or lines either dropping or rising from it, which will also be found to give very remarkable information. For example: if a sloping Line of the Head at any point in its track seems to curve or slightly bend upwards, it indicates that about that period of the person's life some unusual strain will be forced upon him. If this curved line is clearly marked and not interfered with by things that look like blotches in it, the person, although of a completely opposite turn of mind to the practical, will yet rise to the occasion, and for the time

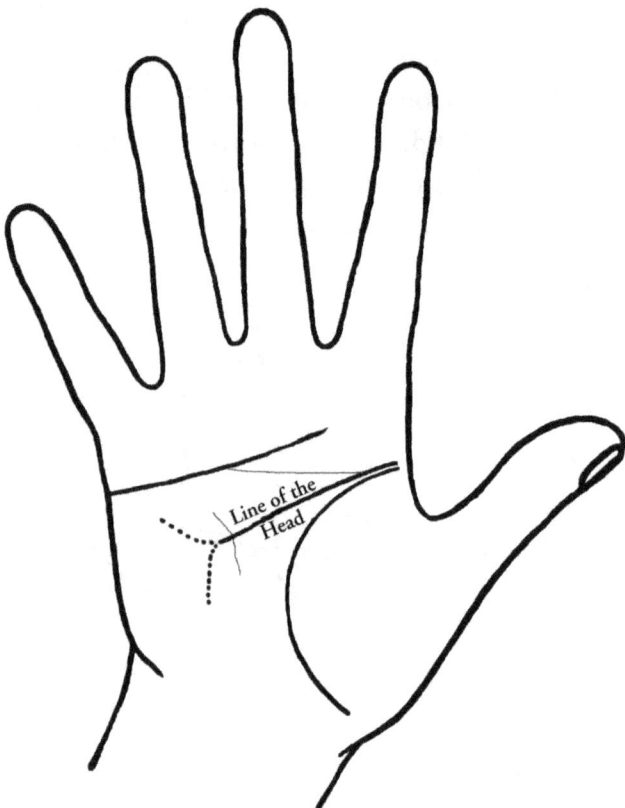

Line of the Head

being will develop a practical or business-like way of looking at things even though it goes against their nature.

If, however, instead of the curve or bend a fine line is seen leaving the Head Line in an upward direction, that period will leave a definite mark on the subject's entire character for the remainder of their life. In some cases these fine lines will, after a few years, appear to develop more strongly, and may even become a kind of second Head Line. This would denote that the person continues to cultivate the practical side of their nature.

If one were examining a straight Line of the Head and noticed a curve downward or a fine line growing downwards from it, the natural interpretation of such a mark would be that at that point in the person's career they had become less practical, or for the time being developed the more imaginative qualities of the mind. In this latter case, curiously enough, it often denotes that the person had at that period of his life become more wealthy or prosperous, and so was able to develop the artistic side of their nature. It is logical to assume that they could only have done this if the strain in the practical battle had been lessened about that time, but this must only be presumed if, at about the same date, the Sun Line were seen clearly marked or suddenly appearing on the hand, then the student can be positive in assuming that at that date greater ease and comfort came into the subject's life and he consequently turned to the more imaginative side of existence.

If the Line of the Head itself should curve upward, especially at the end towards the fourth finger or Mount of Mercury, it denotes, almost without exception, that the longer the person lives the more his desire for money and his determination to possess it will become stronger every year.

If the Line of the Head apparently partly leaves its natural place, which will be seen by an examination of the left hand, and completely rises as it were to the Line of Heart, the person will develop a fixation on one particular goal. He will deliberately control the affectionate side of his nature by his willpower, and will stop at nothing to obtain the realization of whatever this goal may be. If this mark is found on a square thick-set material looking hand, the subject has set his determination on some material object, such as wealth, and he will stop at nothing, even crime, in carrying out their aim. If this mark is found on a long hand the object of the ambition is certain to be connected with intellectual power over people and absolute determination to accomplish whatever the purpose of the career may be.

This mark must not be confounded with one clear line running across the hand from side to side, because in this case the Line of the Head has not risen out of its position, but simply denotes tremendous intensity of character, for good or evil as the case may be; such a person would exhibit great power of concentration, and if he concentrated his mind on any purpose he would unite with it his heart nature. But if he had set his heart or affections on any person, he would unite with that desire the whole force of his mental nature. In this case it is as if these two sides of the mentality, the sentimental and the mental, were linked or in some way united together. Such persons I have always found possess greater intensity of purpose than any other, but I have never found it a very happy mark to possess.

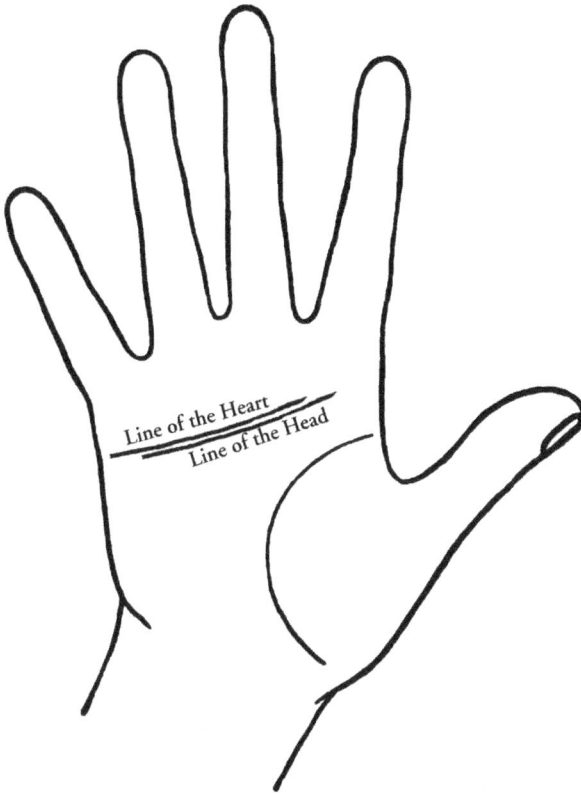

Line of the Heart
Line of the Head

The Head Line and the Heart Line running together

This peculiar type of person appears to be so rare in life that he seems to have no companions and for that reason has always the feeling of being intensely lonely and isolated from others. He is usually also in every way super-sensitive and easily wounded in his feelings. I have seldom found these people successful, unless when acting alone, but if linked with others by partnership in business, etc., they seem to feel their personality cramped, and the partnership as a rule seldom succeeds. In considering this, the student must carefully observe whether this one line across the hand lies across the center where the Head Line would naturally be, or whether it lies higher up towards the base of the fingers where the Heart

Line is generally found. If the former case, one may be sure that it is a question of head and mentality and very little heart; but if the latter, it is a question of more intensity of feeling emotion and affection than of mental intensity.

Crosses and squares on the Line of the Head

Small, sharply-defined crosses in any position just over or touching the Line of Head are generally signs of injuries to the head itself.

Under Jupiter, they usually are brought about by blows caused generally by the subject's desire to rule and to be too dogmatic or tyrannical.

Under Saturn, crosses indicate injuries to the head from attacks by animals, blows by treachery, mine explosions, etc., and generally relate to violence.

Under the Mount of the Sun, these crosses have been found to relate to accidents to the head from sudden falls, such as the subject striking his head by falling, concussion of the brain, etc.

Under the Mount of Mercury, these sharply defined crosses relate to injuries to the head due to injuries generally produced by scientific experiments or some hazardous business venture.

Small defined squares touching the Line of Head, are in all cases signs of preservation, and they relate to the particular qualities of the Mount of the hand under which they are found.

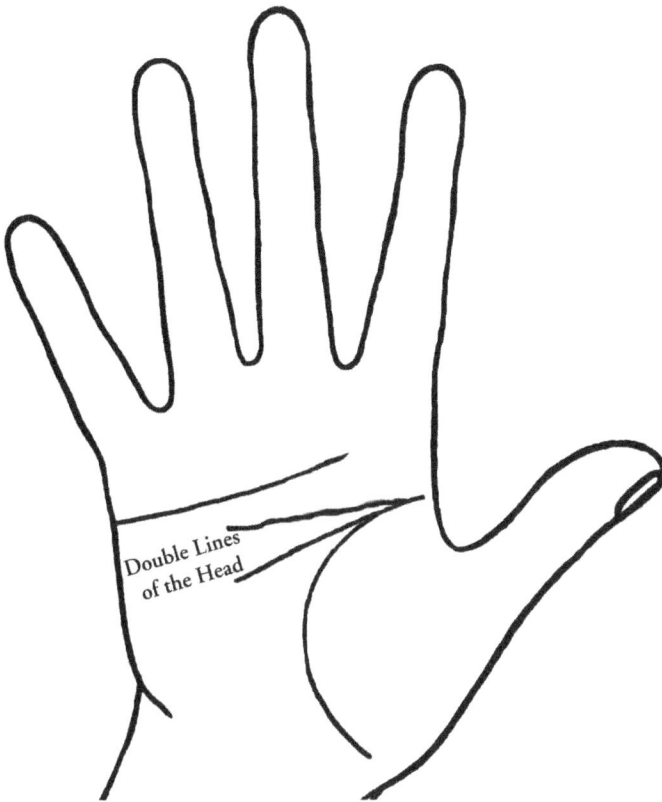

Double Lines of the Head

Double Lines of the Head

Double Lines of the Head, are as rarely found as are cases of the single line right across the hand. In all cases where the double Line of the Head stands out distinct and clear as two separate lines, the object will be found to have a dual mentality. This person is usually capable of an enormous amount of mental work and is of that type of person who can carry out two separate mental lives with success. It is often found with one line joined to the Line of Life and the other rising from the Mount of Jupiter; if such is the case, the interpretation would be that one side of their nature is extremely sensitive and cautious, while the other is self-confident with a great desire to rule or enforce its ideas on the world.

Although such a sign as the double Line of the Head

denotes a remarkable degree of intelligence, I have always found it a better sign to find a single clear Line of the Head, well marked on the hand, instead of two Lines of the Head in any of their positions.

Another form of the double Line of the Head, is one where the main line seems to separate about the middle of the hand, and where one branch goes across the hand and the other descends towards the Mount of the Moon. In such a case we get the double mental personality, but one which is more under the control of the will of the subject, whereas the two double distinct lines denote that the two mental personalities seem to act independently one from the other.

It has been considered by many ancient authorities that the double Line of the Head, when found with two distinct lines, is a sign of the inheritance of great riches or power. I have generally found, however, that what it means is, that although the financial results of such a person's life may be either great wealth or power, yet he may inherit it from his mental right and not from his birth right.

The Line of the Head on the seven types of hands

As a rule the Line of the Head is generally found in accordance with the type of hand on which it is seen, namely, lying straight or what is called "level-headed" on the Square-looking or practical hand; or sloping, and thus indicating the more imaginative qualities on the Philosophic, Conic, or Psychic types.

Consequently, if it be found on a hand in what may be called opposition to its class, such a Line of the Head immediately possesses a greater significance. For example, if a sloping Line of the Head were seen on the Square hand, it would indicate that though the basis of that person's thoughts and plans were of the practical kind, they possessed a far greater power of imagination than any casual observer would at first sight give them credit for.

On the contrary, if the Line of the Head were found straight or level on the Spatulate, Philosophic, Conic, or Psychic types, it would denote that the person in question was usually level-headed and practical, even in their highest dreams of philosophy or idealistic creations.

On the Elementary hand the Line of the Head is usually found short, and straight, often nothing more than a short deep-set furrow. Consequently, if found long and clear, it would indicate a superior mental development than would otherwise be expected from one with such a hand.

If in a Square-looking hand the Line of the Head were found sloping instead of long and straight, it would denote an unusual development of the artistic and imaginative qualities, but always with the practical and logical basis for its support.

On the Spatulate hand the natural position of the Line of the Head is long, clear and sloping, but if found straight or level it would indicate a practical development of the brain endeavoring to offset the originality indicated by the Spatulate formation.

On the Philosophic type, the hand of the thinker and philosopher, the usual position of the Line of the Head is long and sloping, but if found straight or level it indicates a mental development of the logical and practical qualities which might not be expected in such a class or type.

The same rules hold good with the Conic and Psychic, but with what is called the Mixed type, the best Line of the Head to find would be one, long straight and level-looking, because this class, being a mixture as it were of all the others, would require a practical or level-headed mentality to hold its own amid the mixture of tendencies which the last type personifies.

*"He sealeth up the hand of every man;
that all men may know his work."*

Job 37:7

The Line of Life

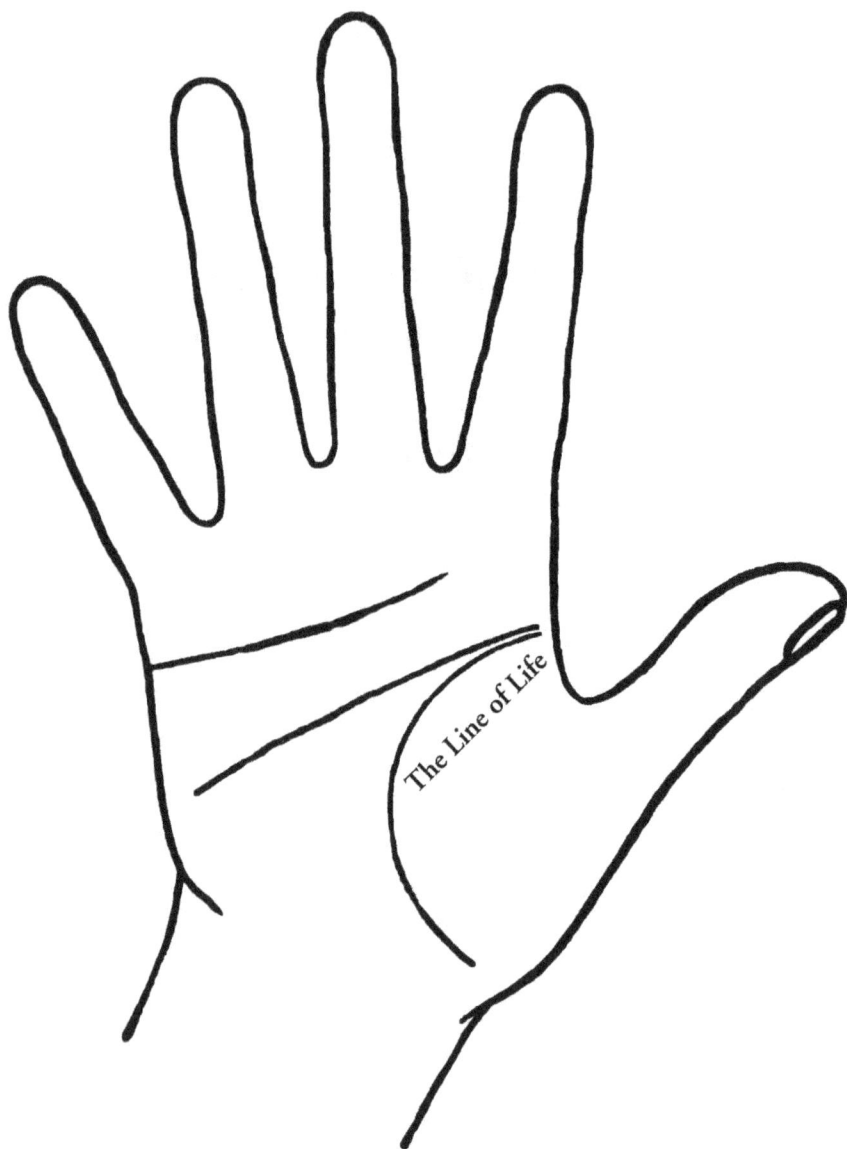

The Line of Life

The Line of Life

6

The Great Palmer Arch

The Line of Life is the line which runs round the base of the thumb and lies directly over a large blood-vessel called the great Palmer Arch. This blood-vessel is connected with the heart, stomach, and vital organs which may have given use to its term "The Vital," as used by the ancients. It is reasonable to assume that it is this intimate connection with the vital organs of the body which enables it to foretell the length of life from natural causes.

The first rule to master is that to be normal the Line of Life should be long, clearly marked, and without any irregularities or breaks of any kind. Such a formation would indicate length of life, vitality, freedom from illness, and strength of constitution.

Defects in the Line of Life

When made up of little pieces or linked like a chain, it is a sign of poor health, weak stomach and lack of vitality. The position of these breaks, marks, links, or islands denotes the portion of the body most affected.

Every line or sign on the hand plays a dual role. By one of their roles these lines indicate the disease the person is most liable to for the entire run of the life, and in another role these lines indicate the date when the illness will reach its greatest gravity. (see chapter on timing)

NOTE: Never predict another person's death, or attempt to diagnose another person's illnesses using palmistry. This information is for your own personal use.

In some hands the Line of Life is broad and shallow on the surface of the hand, in others it is deep and fine; the appearance of this line is very often deceptive, and leads students astray when they have not had their attention called to its appearance.

The broad, shallow Line of Life often leads people to suppose that it is a sign of a very healthy, robust constitution; but, on the contrary, such an indication is not nearly as good a sign as a clear, thin, deep line. The broad Life Line seems to belong to people who have more robust animal strength, whereas the finer line relates to people who have more nerve or will-force. Under any strain of ill-health, it is the finer line that will hold out, whereas the broad-looking line has not the same resisting force.

Very broad lines on the hand denote more muscular strength than will power, and I cannot impress this difference too strongly on the minds of my readers. If the line is made of chain formation it is a sure sign of a tendency to bad health, and especially so if the hand is soft. The same marks on a hard, firm hand would not indicate as much delicacy, because hard, firm hands denote in themselves a robust constitution.

Another important point to consider is, whether the Line of Life goes straight up to the side of the Mount of Venus and narrows that Mount, or whether it forms a well-defined curve or semicircle out into the palm. In the first case it indicates a naturally more delicate constitution, and less force of animal magnetism. People who have a weaker constitution are more likely to have this Mount of Venus (and consequently also the Great Palmer Arch) narrower in construction than those who have a robust constitution and strong circulation of the blood. This is the reason why, when the Mount of Venus is large and wide on the hand, it gives rise to the idea that it indicates a more passionate animal nature than when this mount is thin and narrow.

When the Line of the Head is curved downwards instead of running straight across the palm, that it seems to be more attracted to the qualities indicated by the Mount of Venus and gives more to the imaginative, romantic nature, showing a greater tendency to fall in love, than with people who possess the Line of the Head running straight across the hand, as if it were not attracted to the qualities indicated by the Mount of Venus. It will thus be seen that every point of this study bearing on character can be reasoned out from a logical standpoint.

If the Line of Life is seen to rise high on the hand towards the Mount of Jupiter, the subject has more control over himself, and his life is more governed by the ambitious side of his nature. When, however, the Line of Life rises lower down on the palm, more from the Mount of Mars, it gives less control over the temper. When this sign is noticed, especially in the case of young persons, it will be found that they are more quarrelsome, more disobedient, and have less ambition in connection with their studies.

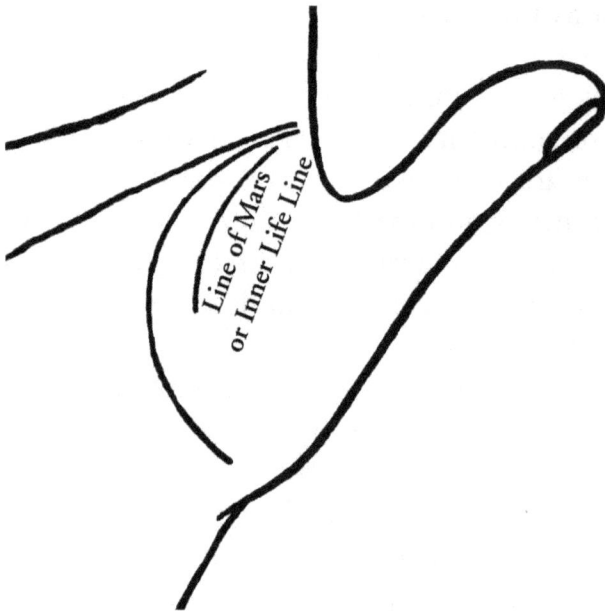

The Line of Mars or the Inner Life Line

The Line of Mars can sometimes be found encircling the Mount of Venus inside the Line of Life. It indicates great vitality and resistance to illness and disease, but is not found on all hands.

This line, which rises on the Mount of Mars, from which it derives its name, when found clear and strong appears to back up and reinforce the Line of Life. It is an excellent sign on the hands of soldiers, or in connection with all persons who follow a dangerous calling.

All breaks or bad marks indicated on the Line of Life are minimized on the hands that have this Inner Life Line, or Line of Mars.

As its name implies, it denotes a robust and rather fighting disposition, a person naturally inclined to rush into dangers and quarrels, and if deeply marked and reddish in color it increases all indications of accidents and dangers shown on other parts of the hand.

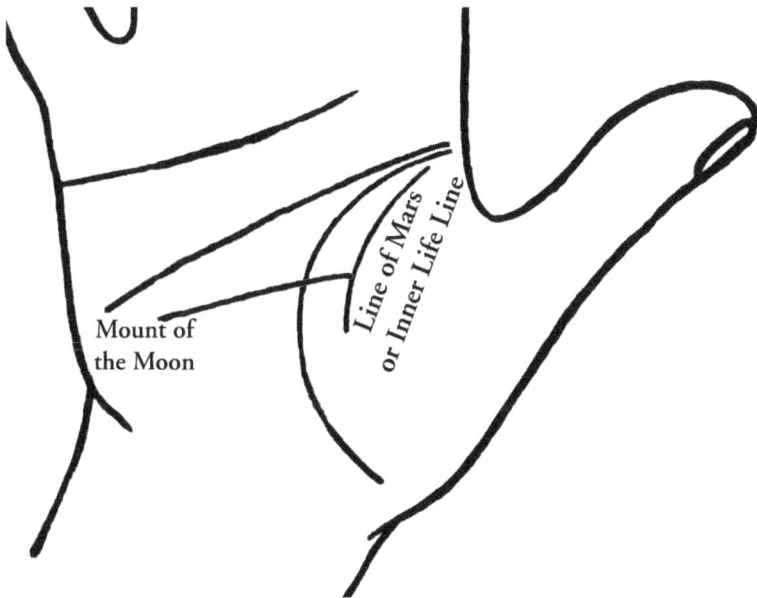

When a branch seems to shoot off from this line and runs on to the Mount of Luna, it foreshadows restlessness and an intense craving for excitement. With a weak-looking Line of the Mind it is a sure sign of a craving for drink and intemperance of all kinds, and at the point where it breaks through the Line of Life, it generally indicates death brought on by the intemperance this mark foreshadows.

It is generally found on short, thick-set square hands or short hands, but when found on a long, thin, and narrow palm, it indicates great vitality and resistance to disease, a nervous, highly-strung, and rather irritable disposition.

Any broken Life Line with this Line of Mars behind it may indicate great danger of death where the break appears, but a danger that will be overcome through the vitality indicated by this Inner Life Line or Line of Mars.

The Line of Fate or Destiny

7

The Line of Destiny, also called the Line of Fate is one of the principal lines of the hand. Although one may never be able to explain why, this line appears to indicate at least the main events of one's career.

It may be found on the hand even at the moment of birth, clearly indicating the destiny that lies in the individual's far distant future.

In some cases it may look faint or shadowy, as if the path of destiny were not yet clearly defined, while in other instances almost every step of the road is chiseled out with its milestones of failure or success, sorrow or joy, as the case may be.

That some human beings seem to be more subject to fate than others has been admitted by almost all thinkers, but why this should be so has been the great question that baffles all students of such subjects.

There are some who appear to have no fate, and others who seem to carve their destiny from day to day. I have seen hundreds of cases where every step of the journey was

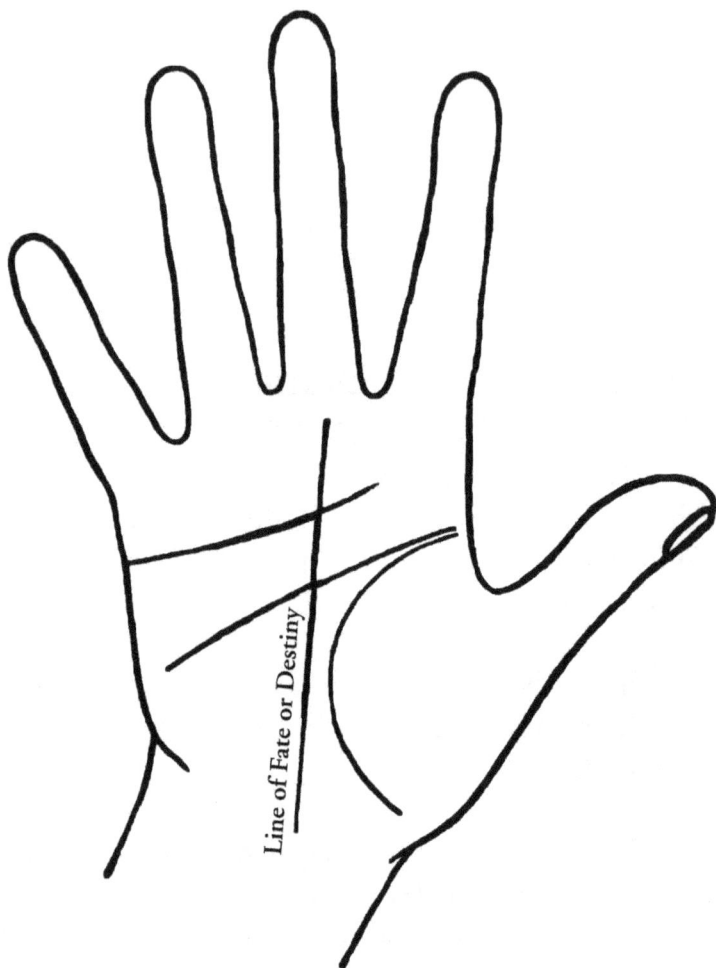

Line of Fate or Destiny

indicated from childhood to the grave; others where only the principal changes in the career were marked in advance. There are, again, others where nothing seemed decided, and where the events indicated by the Line of Fate appeared to change from year to year.

The why and wherefore of such things may be impossible to fathom, but there are so many mysteries in life itself that one more or less does not seem to matter.

Some of the greatest teachers and philosophers have come to the conclusion that fate exists for all. In the 17th Article of Religion in the Episcopal Church it is stated, and in no uncertain manner, that "Predestination to life is the everlasting purpose of God." All through the Bible the destiny of nations and of men is clearly laid down, and from the first chapter of Genesis to the last page of Revelation the trials, tribulations, and pathway of the Jews was prophesied and predicted ages in advance.

Thousands of years before the birth of Christ, it was foretold in Holy Writ in what manner He should be born, and in what manner He should die. It was predicted that a Virgin should conceive and that a Judas should betray, and that both were necessary "that the Scriptures might be fulfilled."

In more recent ages thousands and thousands of predictions have been fulfilled, and all point to some mysterious agency that underlies the purpose of humanity, and that nothing from the smallest to the greatest is left to blind chance.

It may be that the Soul--in being part of the Universal Soul of all things--knows all things, and so through the instrumentality of the brain writes its knowledge of the future in advance.

To the mysteries of the mind there are no limits. There must be an advance growth or change in the brain cells years before action or change in character become the result of such development. For all we know, every deed in our careers is the result of some such mental change, and as there are more super-sensitive nerves from the brain to the hand, it may then follow that such changes and subsequent actions in our lives may be written in our hands even years in advance.

It may be, then, that to all living beings there is a destiny that shapes our lives. All such questions as these the student of this subject must settle in their own mind, for when they once broach this study of fate, they will be assailed on all sides, and the student must be prepared to give an explanation for their belief.

I would, however, suggest that each of us endeavor to find what our fate may be, and like loyal workmen accept whatever the task should prove, and so carry it out to the utmost of our ability, willing to leave the final result to the Master that thought fit to employ us in the working out of His design.

In studying the hand it will be found that the Line of Fate may rise from the following distinct positions: It may rise from and out of the Line of Life, straight up from the wrist, from the Mount of the Moon, or from the middle of the palm.

Rising from the Line of Life

Rising from the Line of Life, the subject's success will be made by personal effort and merit; the early years of such a Fate will be difficult; circumstances and the early surroundings will not be favorable, and such people will be greatly hampered by the wishes and plans of their parents or relatives. If the Line of Fate, however, should run on clear and strong from where it leaves the Line of Life, then the subject will overcome all such difficulties and win success by his own personal effort and merit, and not depend on what is termed luck at any time in their career.

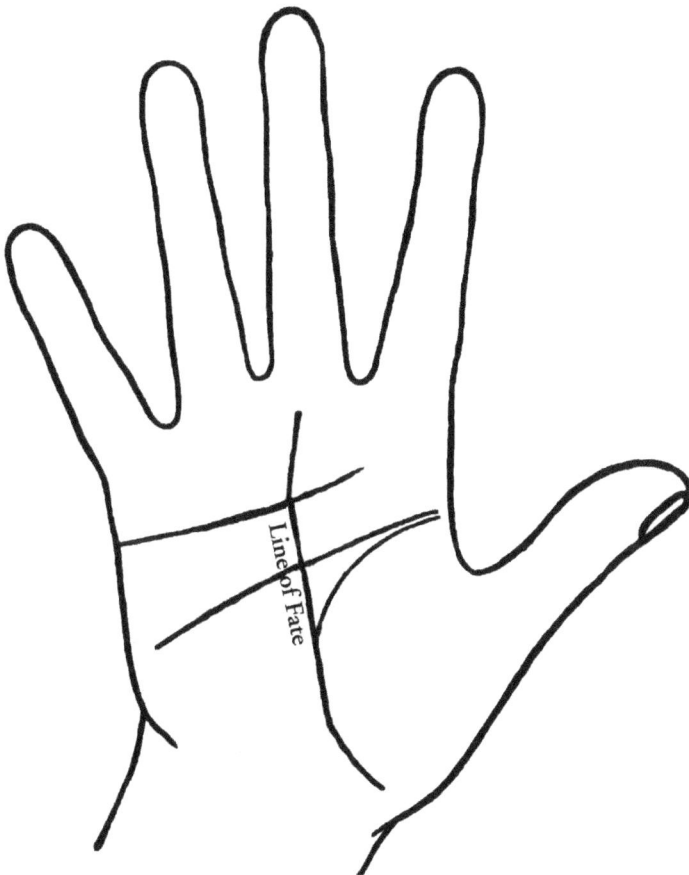

Line of Fate

Rising from the wrist

When the Line of Fate rises from the wrist and goes straight up the centre of the palm to the Mount of Saturn, provided at the same time the Line of Sun is found well marked, luck, brilliance, and success will attend the destiny, and extreme good fortune may be anticipated.

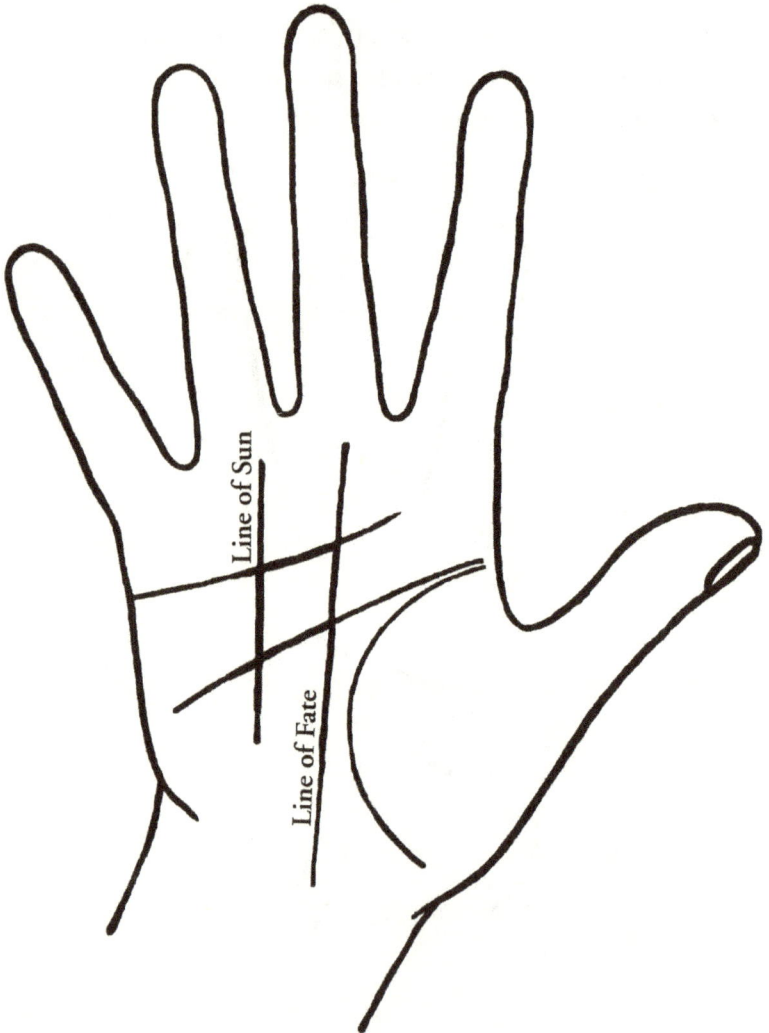

Line of Sun

Line of Fate

Rising from the Mount of the Moon

Rising from the Mount of the Moon the fate will be more eventful, changeable, and largely depending on the fancy and caprice of other people.

If such a line be found joining the Line of Heart, it foretells a happy and prosperous marriage, but one in which idealism, romance, and some fortunate circumstances play their role, and one which results more from the caprice or fancy of the person of the other sex.

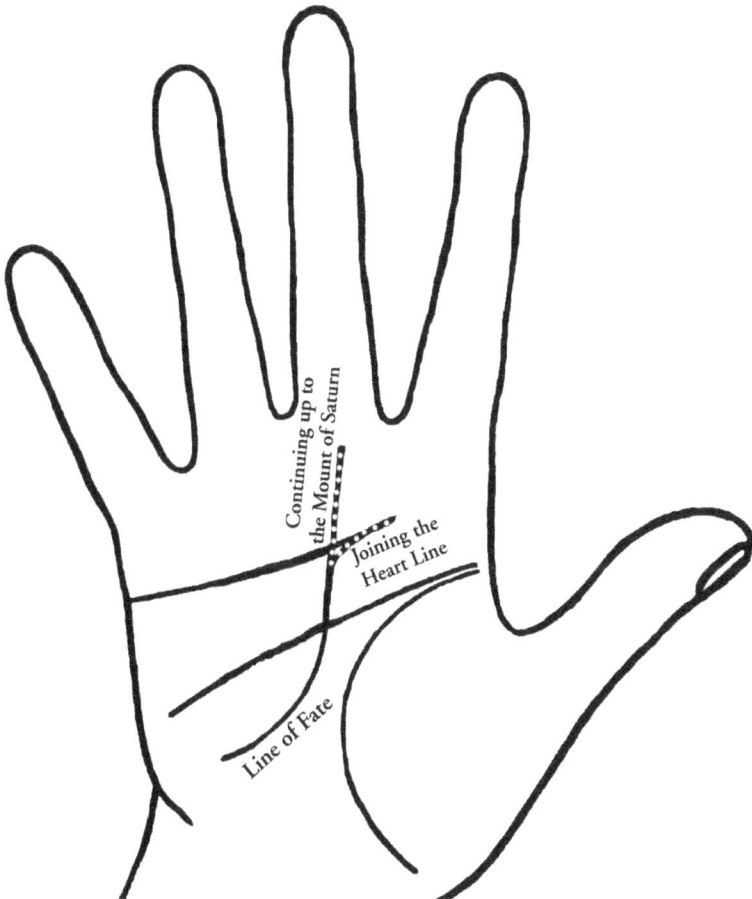

Continuing up to the Mount of Saturn

Joining the Heart Line

Line of Fate

Influence lines

If the Line of Fate be itself straight but with a line running in and joining it from the Mount of the Moon, it indicates that the influence of some outside person has helped the subject's Fate, and it is generally an indication of the influence of another sex to the one on whose hand it appears.

When this line of influence from the Mount of the Moon does not, however, blend with the Fate Line, it denotes that the other person's life will always remain distinct, and the influence will last only for the length of time that it runs by the side of the subject's Fate Line.

When this influence line cuts the Line of Fate and, leaving it, travels on for some distance towards the Mount of Jupiter it tells that the person whose influence it denotes will only be attracted to the subject by personal ambition--that this person will use the subject for the furthering of his own aims and ambitions, and will desert the subject when she is of no further use. This is more commonly seen on the hand of a woman than on that of a man.

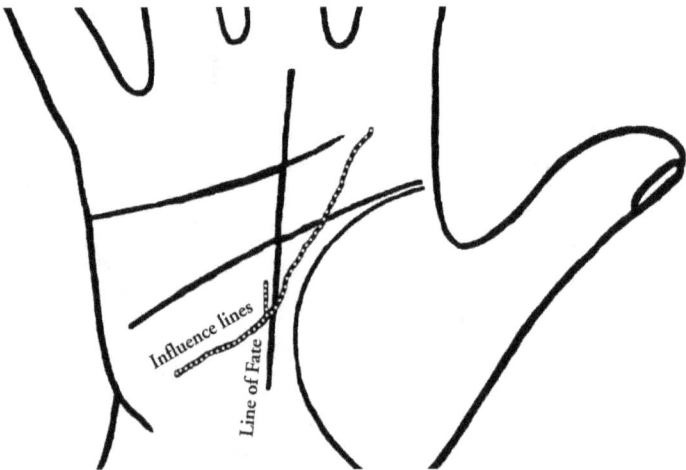

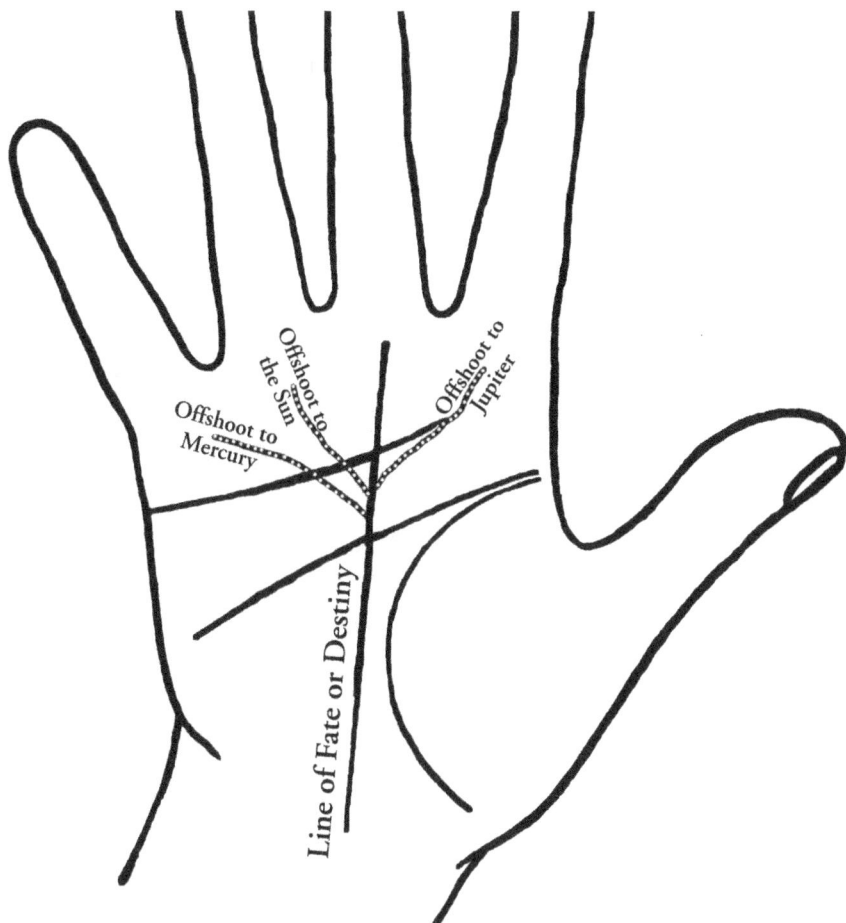

Offshoot to the Sun

Offshoot to Mercury

Offshoot to Jupiter

Line of Fate or Destiny

Offshoots from the Line of Fate

If the Line of Fate ascending the hand sends an offshoot from it on or towards any of the mounts, such as to Jupiter, the Sun, or Mercury, then the Destiny will be more largely associated with the quality that the Mount it approaches symbolizes.

For example: If such a line be seen approaching or going towards Jupiter it denotes responsibility, power of command over others, or some high position which will commence to be realized from the date when the offshoot leaves the Line of Fate. If such a mark continues its course and finishes on the Mount of Jupiter, it is one of the most magnificent signs of success that can be found for that particular aim or purpose.

If this offshoot ascends towards the Mount of the Sun the success will be in the direction of riches and public life, which will give great publicity or renown; this is also a magnificent sign of success.

If the offshoot goes towards the Mount of Mercury the success it indicates will be more in the direction of some special achievement either in science or commerce.

If the Line of Fate itself should not ascend towards its habitual position on the Mount of Saturn, but, instead, run up towards or on to any other Mount, then the whole effort of the life will be tinged with whatever quality that particular Mount signifies. Such an indication must not, however, be considered as the certain or sure sign of success as when the Line of Fate keeps to its own place and sends branches to some particular Mount.

When the Line of Fate ascends the hand without branches and runs like a lonely path up and on to the Mount of Saturn, such a person will be like a child of Fate chained to an iron road of circumstances. It will be impossible for them to avert the trials of their destiny or mitigate them in any way. They will receive no help from others, and little will ever happen except to bring them sorrow or tragedy. Such a mark of fate through the hand must never be considered as a good Line of Destiny.

To have a really good Line of Fate it should not be too heavily marked, but just clear and distinct, and, above all, be accompanied by a Line of Sun in some form or other.

If a Line of Fate runs over the Mount of Saturn and up into the base of the finger, it is an unfortunate sign, as everything the subject undertakes will slip out of his control, and he will not know how or when to stop whatever he takes up.

When the Line of Fate appears to be stopped by the Line of Heart, the career will always be ruined through or by the affections being badly placed.

When, however, it joins the Line of Heart and they together ascend the Mount of Jupiter, the subject will have happiness through his affections and will be helped by love and affection to attain his highest ambitions. He will also be extremely lucky through the friendship and love of those he meets, and will be greatly benefited and helped by others.

When the Line of Fate appears to be stopped by the Line of Head, it foretells that his career will be spoiled by the subject's own foolishness.

Rising from the middle of the palm

When the Line of Fate only makes its appearance far up in the centre of the palm, in what is called the Plain of Mars, it indicates a hard early life and that the subject must always have a hard fight to gain his ends; but should the line ascend clearly and strongly from the Plain of Mars and have a branch to or on towards the Mount of the Sun, such a person will be the architect of his own fortunes, and without help or assistance will win success and fortune by his own personal hard work and merit.

When the Line of Fate rises from the Line of the Head and when it is well marked, everything will come to the subject late in life and only then by his own effort.

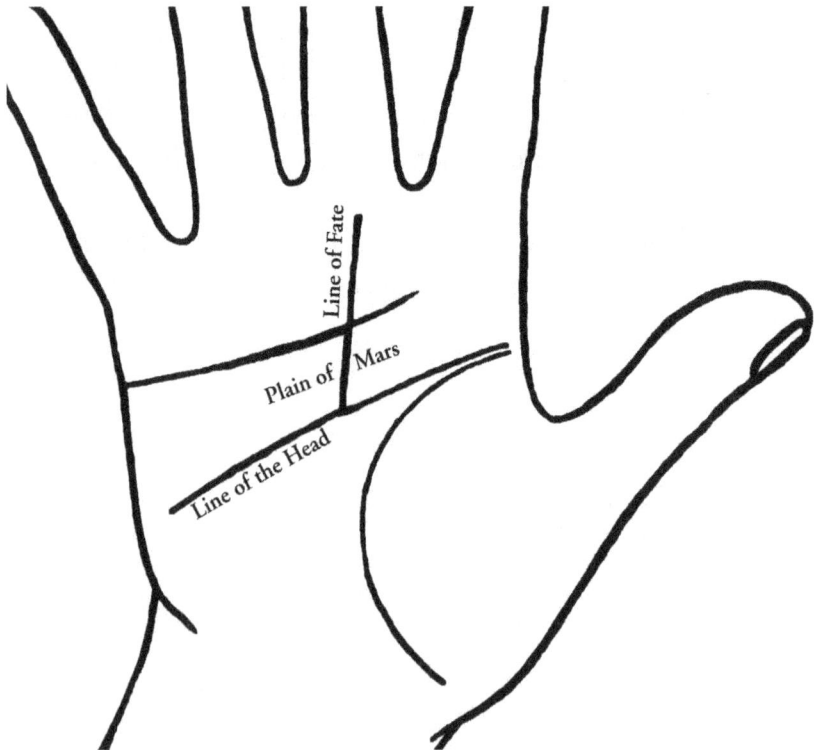

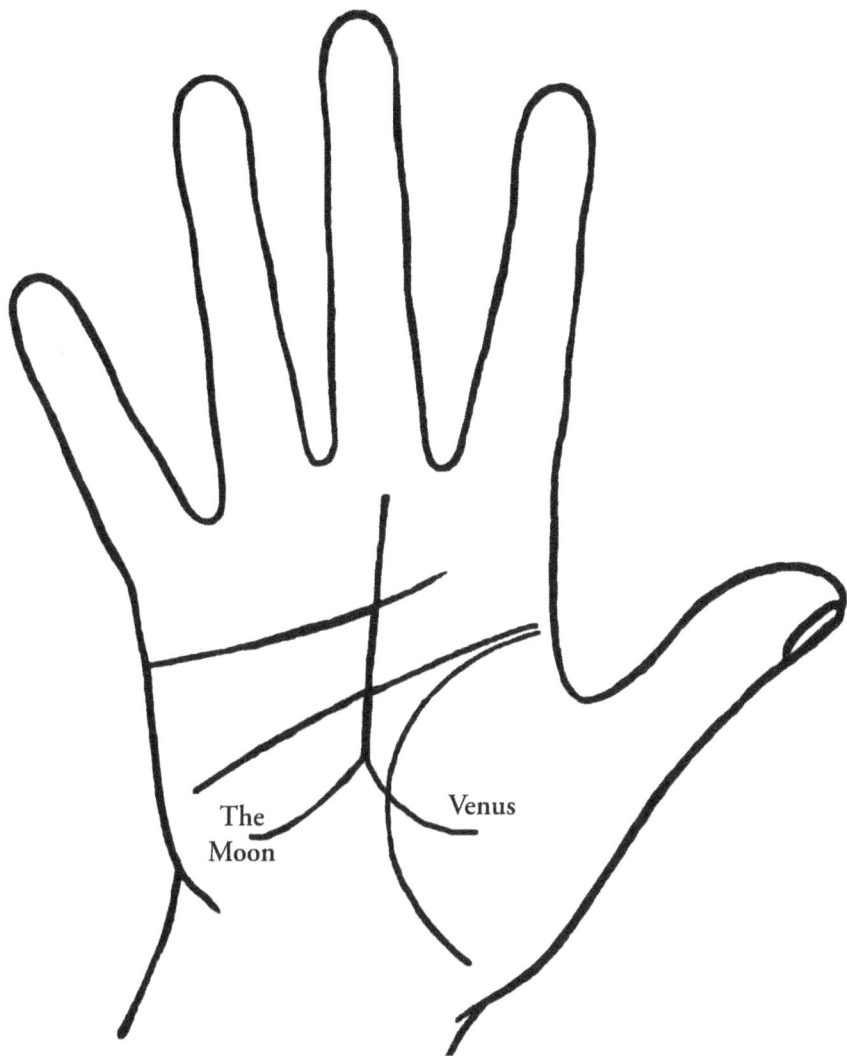

The
Moon

Venus

Branches on Venus and the Moon

When the Line of Fate is seen with one branch on the Mount of Venus and the other on the Mount of the Moon it indicates a career of romance and passion, by which the whole of the destiny will be swayed.

Rising from inside the Life Line

When the Line of Fate itself rises inside the Life Line on the Mount of Venus, passionate love will affect the whole career, and such persons, it will be found, usually place their affections on impossible people or on those who are in some way tied up by marriage or who otherwise are unable to gratify the love that the other person demands. This is a most unlucky sign for affection to find in the hands of a woman.

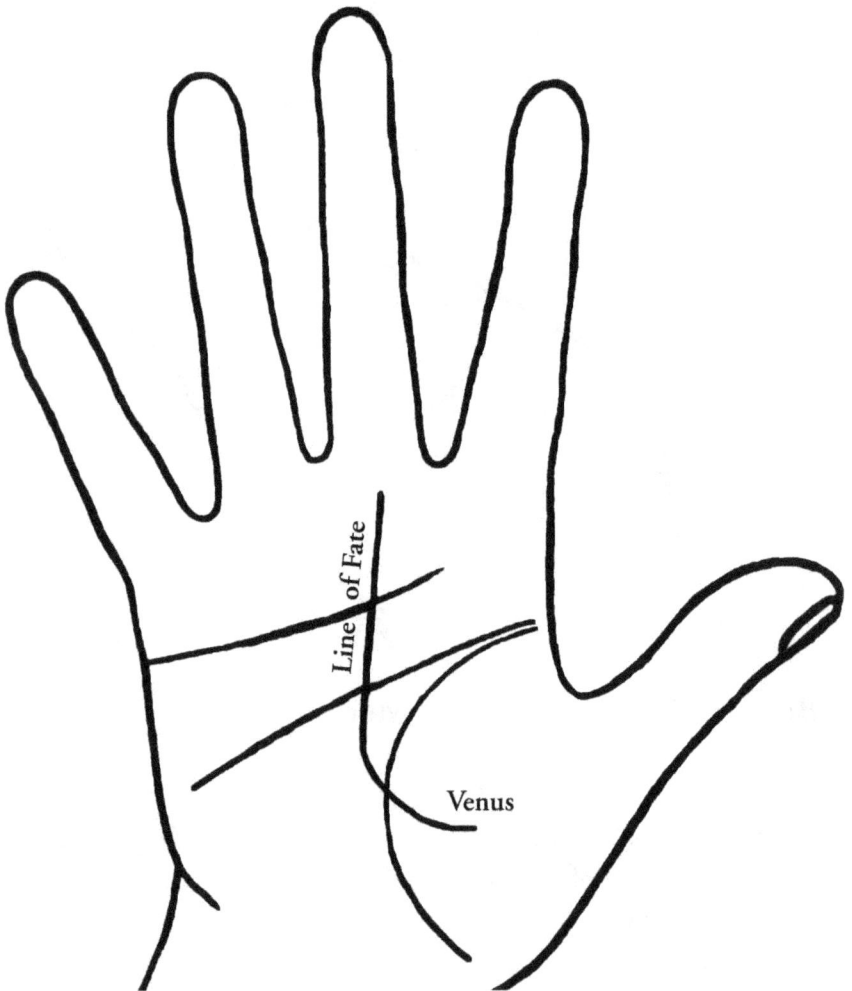

Line of Fate

Venus

Broken Line of Fate

When the Line of Fate is broken or made up in little bits, the career will be found full of troubles, breaks, and nothing that one gets will last long enough to bring any settled or continuous success.

A break in the Fate Line is not always a bad sign to have, provided that one side begins before the other ends; in such a case it foretells a complete change in surroundings and position, and if the new line looks good and straight it will be found to mean that the change will bring about an advancement in position.

Additional influence lines

When any small line joins the Fate Line or goes on with it as an attendant line, such a mark usually indicates marriage at the point when these lines join. If, on the contrary, these lines do not join, marriage with the person is not likely to occur although the affection and influence will be present in the career.

When one of these influence lines appears by the side of the Fate Line and crosses through it towards or on to the Mount of Mars, it indicates that the influence thus shown will turn to hate and will injure the career of the person on whose hand it is found.

Double Line of Fate

When the Line of Fate is itself double, it is a sign of what is called "a double life," but if, after running side by side for some length these two lines join or become one, it foretells that "the double life" has been caused by some great affection, that circumstances prevented a union, but that the preventing cause will be removed at the point where these two lines join.

When, however, a double Line of Fate is clearly marked, especially if they incline towards different mounts of the hand; such a mark indicates that two careers would be carried out simultaneously--one perhaps as a hobby and the other as the principal career.

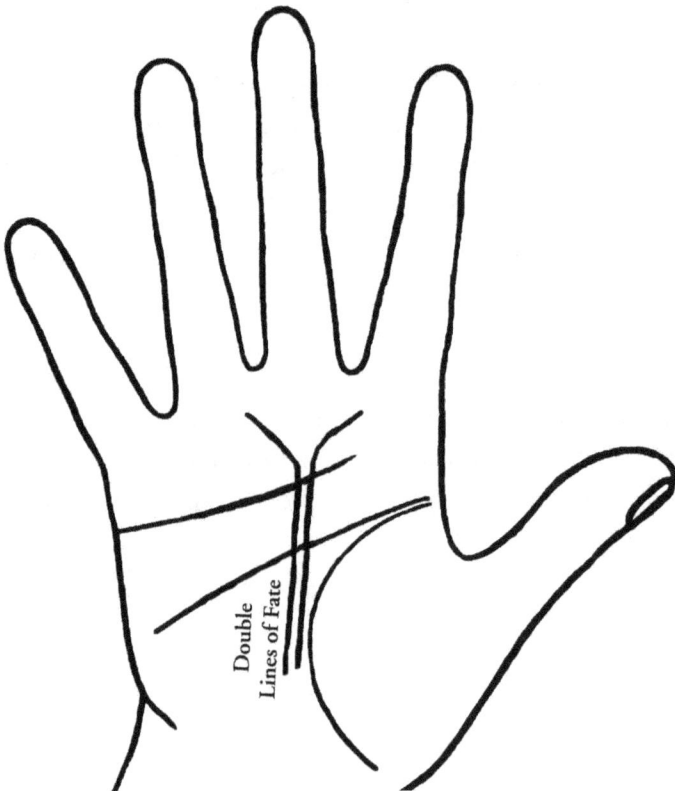

Double Lines of Fate

Defects in the Line of Fate

When the Line of Fate is extremely faint or just barely traced through the palm, it will be found to indicate a general disbelief in the idea of fate and destiny. It is often found on the hands of very materialistic persons, those who rebel against the idea that they are governed in any way by fate or by any power save themselves.

When this is found along with a good clear Line of the Head, such people will be sure to win success by their mentality alone, but the details of their destiny will not be able to be told, and one must content oneself with chiefly describing their characteristics, peculiarities, etc.

When no Line of Fate whatever is found and only a very ordinary Line of the Head, then there will be nothing very particular to say about the destiny; such people, as a rule, lead very colorless lives, nothing seems to affect them much one way or the other, and they will be found to have very little purpose to illumine the drab monotony of their existence.

Islands on the Line of Fate

An island is an extremely bad sign to find in the Line of Fate. When found at the very beginning of the line it indicates some mystery regarding the commencement of such careers, such as illegitimate birth.

An island, when found on a woman's hand connecting the Fate Line with the Mount of Venus, is an almost certain indication of her seduction.

An island in any part of the Plain of Mars indicates a period of great difficulty, loss in one's career, and in consequence, generally loss of money.

An island on the Fate and Head Lines together means loss also, but more brought on by the person's own foolishness or lack of forethought.

An island over the Fate and Heart Lines indicates loss and trouble connected with affairs of the heart.

An island on the Mount of Saturn or towards the end of the Line of Fate foreshadows that the career will finish in poverty and despair.

When the Line of Fate finishes suddenly with a cross, some great fatality may be expected, but when the cross is found on the Fate Line and on the Mount of Saturn, the ending of such a destiny will be some terrible tragedy, generally one of public disgrace and public death.

8

The Line of the Heart

The affectionate or emotional nature

The Line of the Heart runs across the hand under the fingers and generally rises under the base of the first finger, and runs off the side of the hand under the base of the fourth or little finger.

The Line of the Heart relates purely to the affectionate disposition, in fact, to the mental side of the love nature of the subject. It should be borne in mind that, by lying as it does on that part of the hand above the Line of Head, it is consequently on the portion of the hand that relates to mental characteristics and not to the physical.

The Line of the Heart should be deep, clear, and well colored. It may arise from the extreme outside of the Mount of Jupiter from the centre of this mount, from the space between the first and second fingers, from the face of the Mount of Saturn, or from directly under this mount.

From the Mount of Jupiter

From the outside of the Mount of Jupiter, it denotes the blind enthusiast in affection, a man or woman who places his or her ideal of love so high that neither fault nor failing is seen in the person being worshipped. With these people their pride in the object of their affection is beyond all reason, and all such extremists as a rule suffer terribly through their affections.

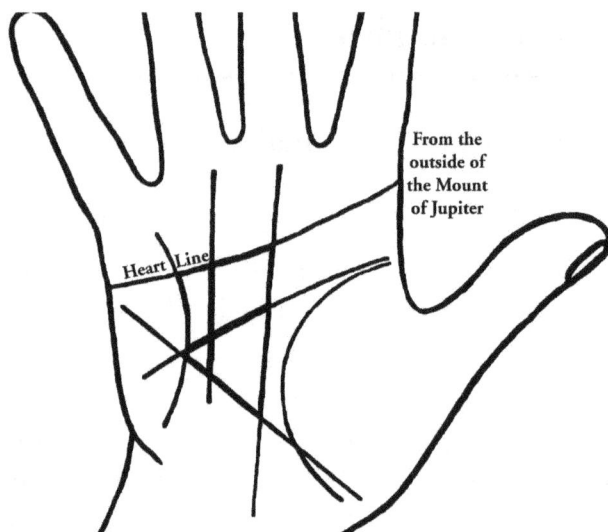

From the outside of the Mount of Jupiter

Heart Line

From the centre of the Mount of Jupiter, the Heart Line gives more moderation, but also great ideality, and is one of the best variations of this Line that we are about to consider.

People with such a Heart Line are firm and reliable in their affections, they have an unusually high code of honor and morality. They are ambitious that the person they live with be great, noble, and successful. They seldom marry beneath their station in life, and they have fewer love affairs than any other class. If they once really love, they love for ever. They do not believe in second marriages, and the divorce courts are seldom troubled with their presence.

The Heart Line rising from between the first and second fingers gives a calmer but a very deep nature in all matters of the affections. These people seem to strike the happy medium between the ideality and pride given by Jupiter, and the more selfish love nature given when the line rises from Saturn.

They are not very demonstrative when in love, but they are capable of the very greatest sacrifices for those they care for. They do not expect the person on whom they bestow their affection to be a god or a goddess.

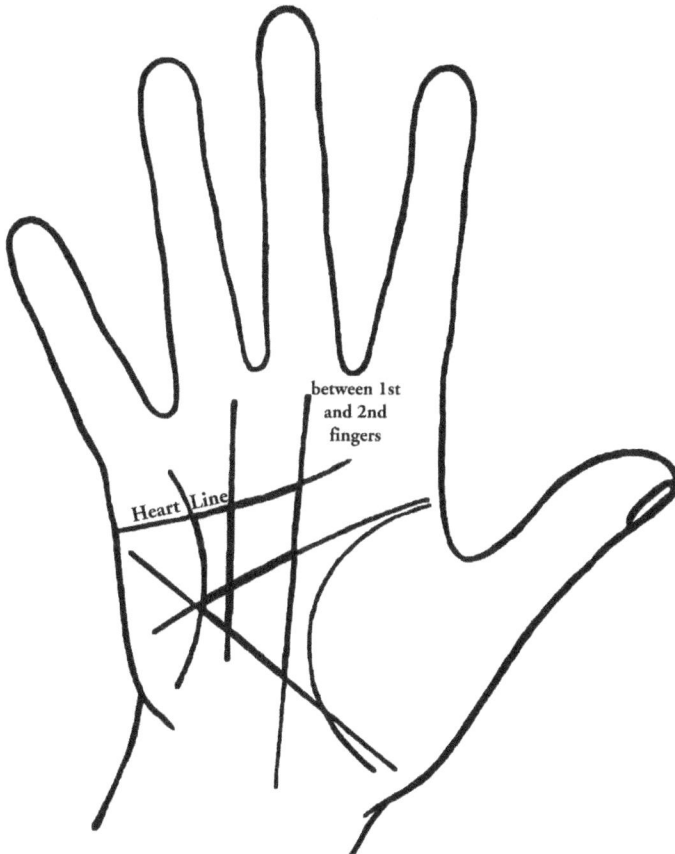

between 1st and 2nd fingers

Heart Line

From the Mount of Saturn

When the Line of the Heart rises on the Mount of Saturn the subject will be rather selfish in all questions of affection. These people are not self-sacrificing, like the previous type. They are inclined to be cynical, reserved, undemonstrative but very insistent in trying to gain the person they want. They will let nothing stand in their way, but once they have obtained their object they show little tenderness or devotion.

They are very unforgiving if they discover any lapses on the part of their partner, but as they are "a law unto themselves," they close their eyes to their own shortcomings.

The Line of the Heart that rises from under the base of the Mount of Saturn, exhibits all the foregoing characteristics, but in a much more intensified form. Such persons live for themselves and care little whether those around them are happy or not.

Defects in the Line of the Heart

The shorter the Line of the Heart is on the hand, the less affectionate the individual will be.

When the Line of the Heart is found in excess, namely, extremely long-it denotes a terrible tendency toward jealousy, and this is alarmingly increased if the Line of Head on the same hand is very sloping towards the Mount of the Moon. In such a case the imagination will run away with itself where jealousy is concerned.

When the Line of the Heart is found curving downward at the base of the Mount of Jupiter, it tells of a strange fatality in that person, of meeting with great disappointment in love, and even with those they trust in friendship. This person seems to lack perception in knowing whom to love. Their affections are nearly always misplaced or never returned.

These people have, however, as a rule, wonderfully kind, affectionate dispositions. They have little pride about whom they love and they generally marry beneath their station in life.

A Line of the Heart made up like a chain, or by a crowd of little lines running into it, denotes flirtations and inconstancy in the love nature, and seldom has any lasting affection.

A Line of the Heart from Saturn in holes or links like a chain, especially when it is broad, denotes an absolute contempt for the opposite sex.

When this Heart Line is pale and broad, without any depth, it denotes a nature blasé and indifferent with no depth of affection.

When very low down on the hand, almost touching the Line of the Head, the heart will always interfere with the affairs of the head.

When it lies very high on the hand and the space is narrowed only by the Head Line being abnormally high and out of its place, it indicates the reverse of the above, and that the affairs of the heart are ruled by the head. Such persons are extremely calculating in all matters of love.

When only one deep, straight line is found across the hand from side to side, the two lines both Head and Heart appear to blend together. This denotes an intensely self-concentrated nature. If such a subject loves, he unites with it all the forces of his mind, and if he puts his mind to work on any subject, he throws his whole heart and soul into whatever it may be.

These people are also terribly head-strong and self-willed in all they do. They do not seem to know what fear means in any sense--they are dangerous lovers and husbands to trifle with, for they will stop at nothing if their blood is once roused. They are also dangerous to themselves. They rush blindly into danger.

When the Line of the Heart commences with a fork, one branch on Jupiter and the other between the first and second fingers, it is an excellent sign of a well-balanced, happy, affectionate disposition, and a good promise of great happiness in all matters of affection.

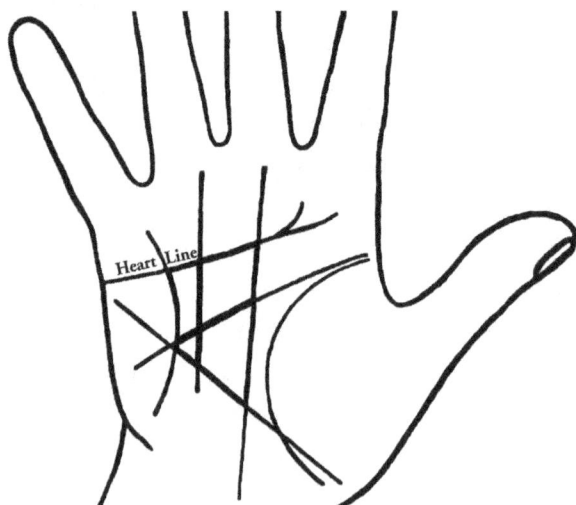

Heart Line

When the Line of the Heart is very thin and with no branches, it denotes coldness and want of heart.

When there is no Line of the Heart whatever, it is a sign of a cold-blooded, unemotional nature. Such people can, however, be brutally sensual and especially so if the Mount of Venus is high.

A broken Heart Line is a certain sign that some terrible tragedy in the affections will at some time or other overwhelm the subject. It may not often be found nowadays, but I have seen it in a few cases, and these persons never recovered from the loss of their loved one or ever had love in their lives again.

"Real success is finding your lifework in the work that you love."

David McCullough (1933 -)
US biographer & historian

The Line of the Sun

9

The Line of the Sun, is also called the Line of Success. It has in its symbolism almost the same significance as the Sun itself has to the Earth. Without this line life has no happiness, no sunshine, as it were, and even the greatest talents lie in darkness and do not produce their fruit.

Amateurs, in looking at hands, often make the greatest mistakes in seeing what appears to be a good Line of Fate, and in consequence rush off and predict great success and fortune, whereas, as I explained in the preceding chapter, a Fate Line unaccompanied by the Line of Sun may simply mean a fatalistic life full of sorrow and darkness.

A "lucky" hand

The Line of the Sun denotes what is generally called "luck". With a well-marked Sun Line even a poor Line of the Head promises more success, and it is the same with the Line of Fate.

People with the Sun Line appear to have more magnetism, more influence over others. They more easily secure recognition, reward, riches, and honors. They also have a happier and brighter disposition, and this has naturally a great deal to do with what is called success.

Where does the "luck" start?

From whatever date in the hand the Line of Sun appears, things become brighter, more prosperous and important. (see chapter on timing) The Line of the Sun may rise from the following positions:

From the Line of Life, the Line of Fate, the Plain of Mars, the Mount of the Moon, the Line of Head, and from the Line of Heart, or it may only appear as a small line on its own Mount.

Rising from the Line of Life, it promises success in life through ones own efforts, but not from "luck."

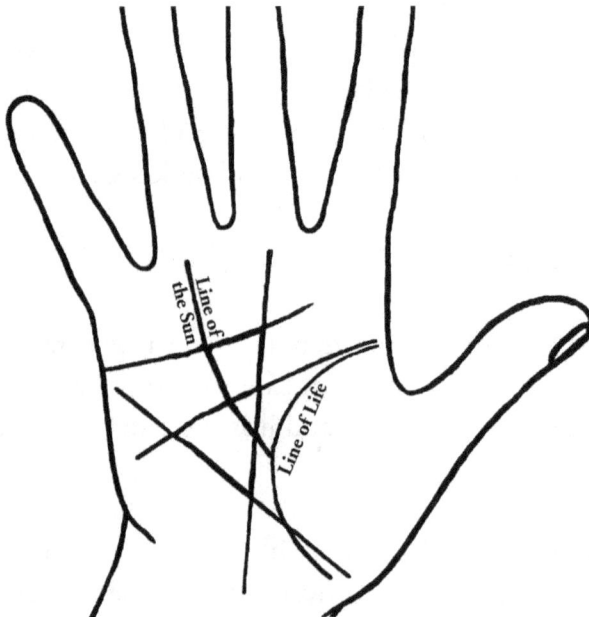

From the Line of Fate, it is a sign of recognition for the career adopted as a result of the personal effort of the subject.

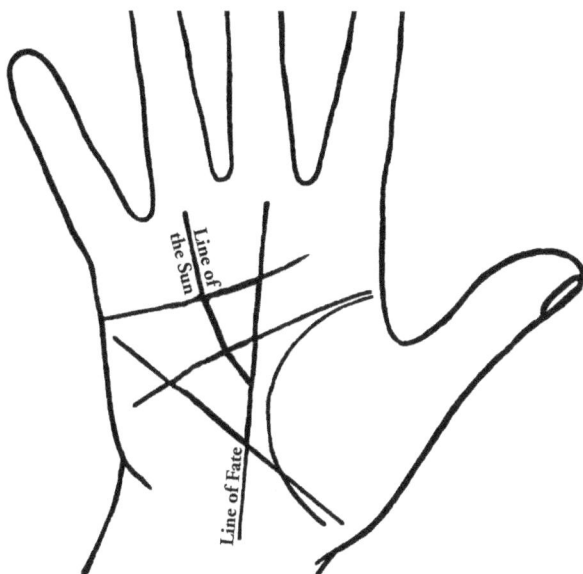

From the Plain of Mars, and not connected with the other lines, it foretells success after difficulties.

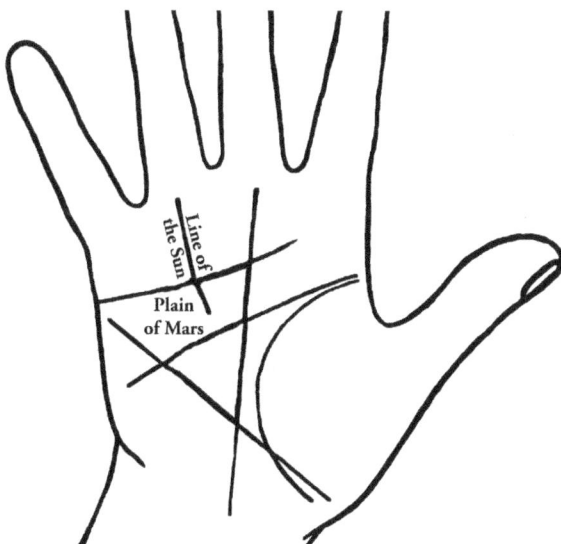

From the Mount of the Moon, success is more a matter due to the caprice of others. It is more changeable and uncertain and is by no means a sure sign of riches or solid position.

It is more the sign of success as a public favorite, and is often found in the hands of those who depend on the public for their livelihood, such as actors, singers, artists, speakers, clergymen, etc. For all such professions it is an extremely lucky sign to have as it promises luck and recognition in the world.

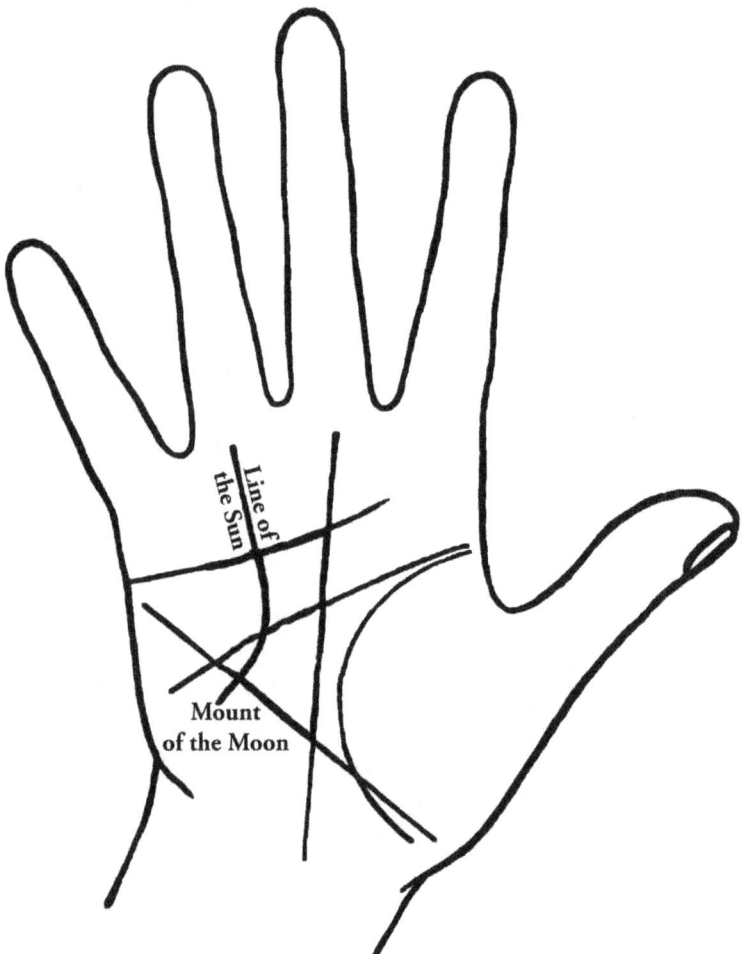

Line of the Sun

Mount of the Moon

Rising from the Line of the Head, the Sun Line gives success from mental efforts and qualities, but not until after middle age. It is found on the hands of people who work with their mind such as writers, scientists, etc.

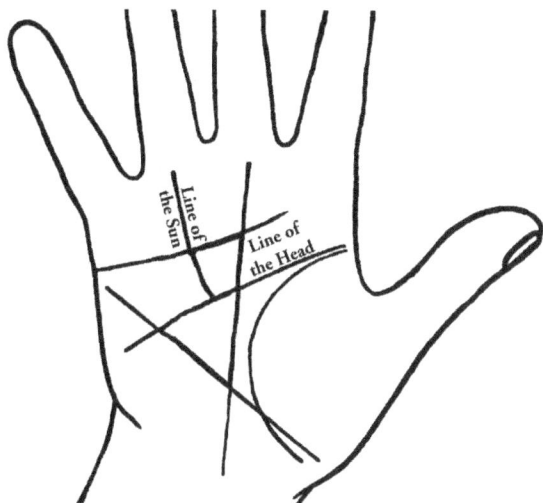

From the Line of Heart, success will come late in life in some way depending on, or through affections. In such cases it generally promises a very happy marriage late in life, but it is always a certain sign of eventual ease, happiness, and worldly comfort.

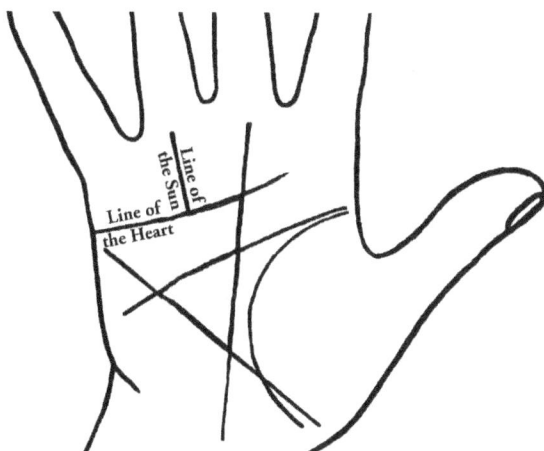

Marked only on its own mount, the Line of Sun promises happiness and success, but so late in life as to make it hardly worth having.

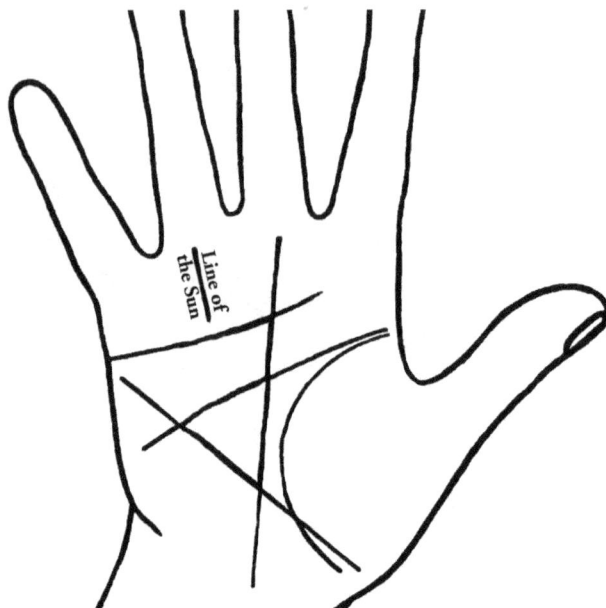

When the third finger--called the finger of the Sun--is much longer than the first with the Line of Sun well marked, the gambling instincts will be much in evidence. Nearly all successful gamblers for money have these two indications.

When, however, the third finger is equal to the second, the love of amassing wealth will be the dominant passion of the life.

When the third finger is extremely long and twisted or crooked, the person will endeavor to obtain money at any cost. This malformation is often seen in the hands of thieves or criminals who are likely to commit any crime for the sake of money. Note--if the Line of Head is very high on the palm, and more especially if it rises upwards at the end these evil qualities will be even more accentuated.

When a hand is found to be artistic in its shape, with pointed fingers or long and narrow, the Line of Sun on such a formation promises success in art, on the stage, or in public life.

The real musician's hand, such as the composer's or player's, is however rarely a long, thin-shaped hand, because such persons must have a more scientific nature. This quality is not found with those who possess the long, slender, very artistic-shaped hand, who depend more on their emotional temperament than on scientific study for their foundation.

On extremely long, thin hands, those that belong to what is called the Psychic type, the Line of Sun has very little meaning except that of temperament, such persons being too idealistic to care for either wealth, position, or worldly success. They have, as a rule, bright, happy, sunny dispositions if this line is marked on their hands, and they go through life as in a dream, and their dreams are to them the only things that matter.

Sensitive people

A curious characteristic, however, is that on all hands where the Sun Line is seen, the nature of such people is much more sensitive to environment than that of those persons who do not possess this line. For this reason the Sun Line has been considered a sign of an artistic nature. But what is known as an artistic nature may show itself only in the love of beautiful things, and harmony of surroundings; whereas the people who do not possess any mark of the Sun Line seldom even notice their surroundings and would live equally happy in the most squalid homes. They would not care whether their curtains were black, green, yellow, or some fearful combination of all three.

When many lines are found on the Mount of the Sun, they show also an artistic nature, but one where the multiplicity of aims and ideas will prevent any real success.

Two or three Sun Lines, when running parallel and evenly together, are good and indicate success in two or three different lines of work; but one good, straight, clear line is the best sign to have.

Opposition lines

An "island" on any part of the Line of the Sun destroys the position and success promised, but only when the island appears. In nearly all cases it denotes public scandal.

All opposition lines, those that cross over from the thumb side of the hand, and especially those from the Mount of Mars or from its direction, are bad. If these opposition lines pass through, cut, or interfere with the Line of Sun in any way, they denote the jealousy or interference of people.

It is interesting to note that these opposition lines from the Mount of Mars relate to the interference of members of the same sex as the subject; while, if they come from the Mount of Venus, they relate to the opposite sex of the individual on whose hand they appear.

A "star" found on the Line of Sun is one of the luckiest and most fortunate signs to have.

A "square" is a sign of preservation against the attacks of enemies or efforts to assail one's position.

A "cross" is an unfortunate sign, and denotes difficulties and annoyance, but only relating to one's name or position.

On a "hollow hand," the Line of Sun loses all power, and its good promises are never fulfilled.

The complete absence of the Line of Sun on an otherwise well-marked hand, indicates that no matter how clever or talented these people may be, the recognition of the world will be difficult or even impossible to gain. In other words, their life will remain in darkness; people will not see their work and the "Sun of Success" will never dawn on their pathway of labor.

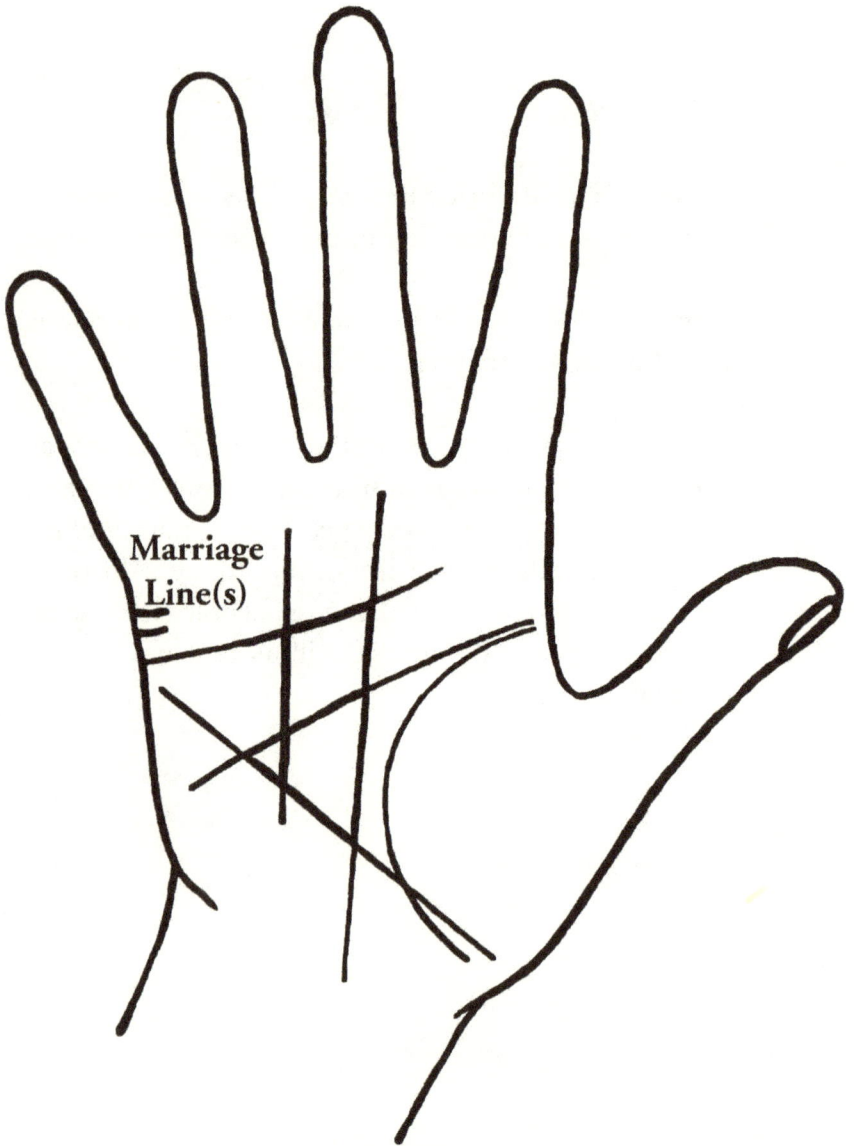

Marriage
Line(s)

Marriage & Children

10

Signs Relating to Marriage

The Line of Marriage is that mark or marks, as the case may be, found on the side of the mount under the fourth finger. The Line of Marriage may be found as very short marks almost on the very side of the hand, or they may appear as quite long lines rising from the side of the hand into the face of the Mount of Mercury, or, in some cases, going farther still into the hand itself.

Only the clearly formed lines relate to marriage, the short ones relate to deep affection, or marriage contemplated, but never entered into. When the deep line is found lying close to the line of Heart, the marriage will take place early in life.

For a happy marriage the lines on the Mount of Mercury should be straight and clear, without breaks or irregularities of any kind.

When the Line of Marriage curves or droops downwards, the person on whose hand this appears will outlive the other.

When the line is clear and distinct, but has a lot of little lines dropping from it, it foreshadows trouble and anxiety in the marriage, but brought on by the delicacy and ill-health of the partner.

Note: Never predict someone's death or suggest that they will have health problems.

When the line has a curve at the end, and if a cross or line be found cutting into this curve, the partner will die by accident or a sudden illness of some kind. But when the Marriage Line ends in a long, gradual curve into the Heart Line, the death of the partner will come about by gradual ill-health or illness of a very long duration.

When the line has an "island" at the beginning, then the marriage will be for a long time delayed, and the two persons will be much separated at the commencement of their married life.

When the "island" is found about the middle of the Marriage Line, some great trouble and separation will take place about the middle of the married life.

When the "island" is found towards the end of the line, the marriage will most probably end in trouble and separation one from the other.

When the Line of Marriage divides into the form of a fork, the two people will live apart from one another, but when the fork turns downwards towards the Line of Heart a legal separation may be anticipated.

When this fork is more accentuated, and turns down more into the hand, divorce may be expected, and especially so if one end of this fork stretches across the hand in the direction of the Plain of Mars, or the Mount of Mars.

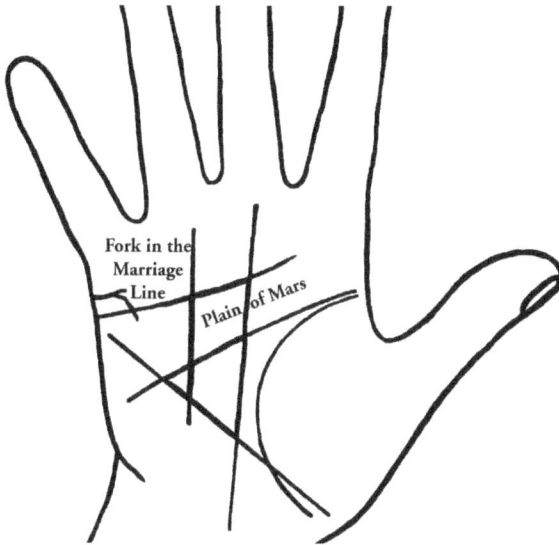

In many cases a fine line may be found crossing the entire palm, from the Marriage Line, and in such a case great animosity and bitterness will enter into the fight for freedom and divorce. In such an example there is never any hope of reconciliation.

When the Line of Marriage is full of little islands, or linked like the loops of a chain, the subject should be warned not to marry, as such a union would be full of the greatest unhappiness and continual separations.

When the line, which is otherwise well marked, appears about the centre to break in two, it foreshadows a fatality or break-up in an otherwise happy married life.

When the Line of Marriage itself, or an offshoot from it, goes into the hand, and joins or ascends upward with the Line of Sun, it promises that its possessor will marry someone of great wealth or distinction.

When this above-mentioned line bends downward and cuts the Line of Sun, it denotes that the person on whose hand it is found will lose their position by the marriage they will make.

When any line from the top of the Mount of Mercury falls down into the Marriage Line, it shows that there will be great obstacles to overcome in whatever marriage the subject enters, but if the Line of Marriage is a good one, then such obstacles will be overcome.

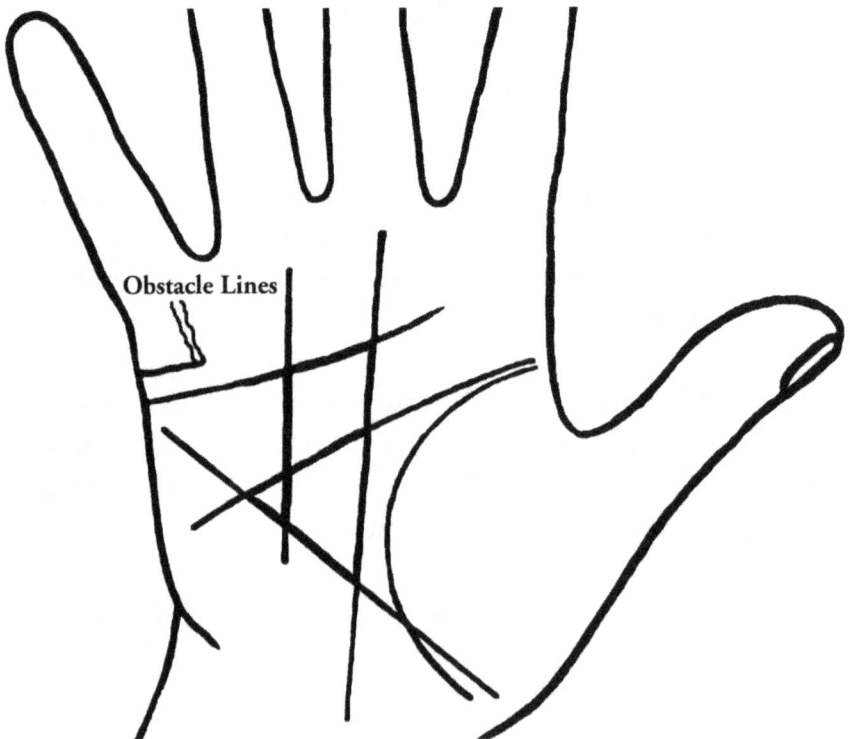

Obstacle Lines

When there is another line much slighter in appearance lying close to the upper side of the Marriage Line, it foretells some influence that will come into the subject's life after marriage.

All lines that cross the hand from the Mount of Mars, and rise up towards the Line of Marriage denote the interference of people with the marriage. These lines give the date of the interference when they cross the Line of Destiny (see chapter on timing). They cause quarrels when they come from Mars. When they come from Venus they also denote annoyances, but not of such a vindictive nature.

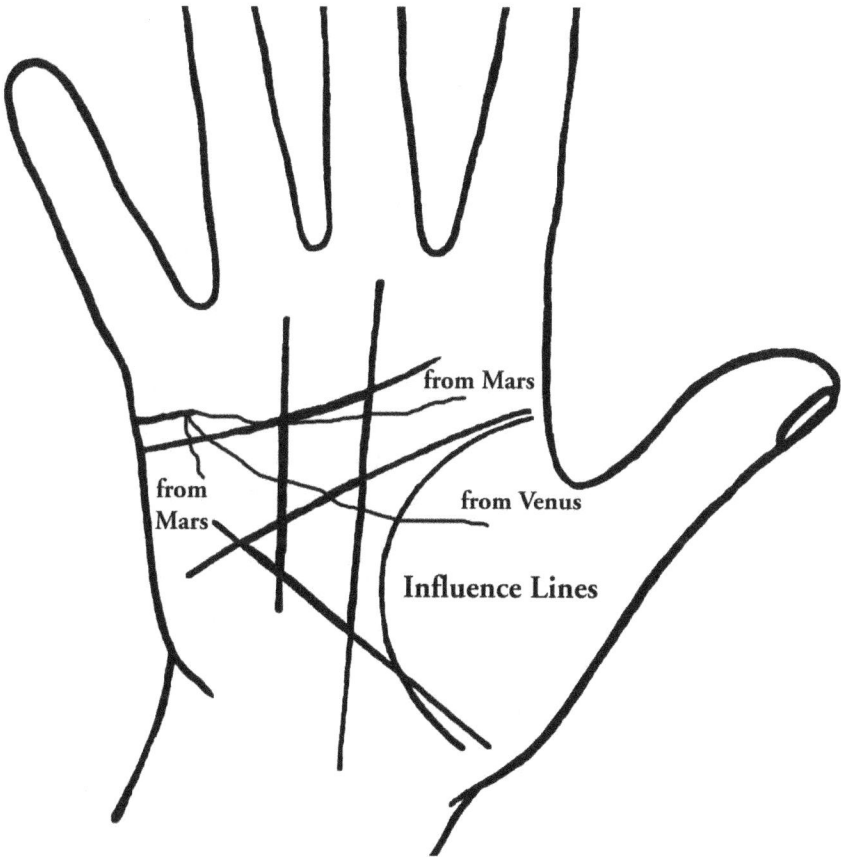

from Mars

from Mars

from Venus

Influence Lines

Other signs which have connections with marriage

The student may also get very great help in ascertaining details about the likely marriage of the person whose hands he is examining by noticing any fine influence lines seen joining the Line of Fate. These lines relate to persons who come into and affect the destiny.

If the influence line is very strong where it joins the Fate Line, and if a clear Marriage Line is seen on the Mount of Mercury, the date of marriage may be more accurately predicted by the place on the Fate Line where the influence line joins it (see chapter on timing).

Influence lines on the Mount of the Moon

Coming over from the Mount of the Moon, there is always something romantic about the union. The person on whose hand this line appears will as a rule meet his love when traveling or away from his home.

If the influence line has an "island" marked on it, the influence will then be a bad one, or, at least, the person will have had some scandal connected with his or her past life. If the Line of Fate looks weaker or more uncertain after the union is marked, then such a marriage has not brought good or success to the subject. If, on the contrary, the Line of Fate looks better or stronger after the influence line has joined it, then this union will prove of advantage to the person whose hand is being examined.

This increase of wealth or power is still more accentuated if at the same time a Sun Line is visible.

If the influence line should cut through the Fate Line, and appear on the thumb side of it, the affection will seldom last as long, or be so happy. If a still wider separation of the influence line and the Fate Line appear as these two lines ascend the hand together, the separation of interests and destiny of the two persons will be still more marked as the years proceed.

If an influence line approaches close to the Line of Fate, and runs parallel with it for some time but does not join it, some great obstacle will prevent a marriage ever taking place.

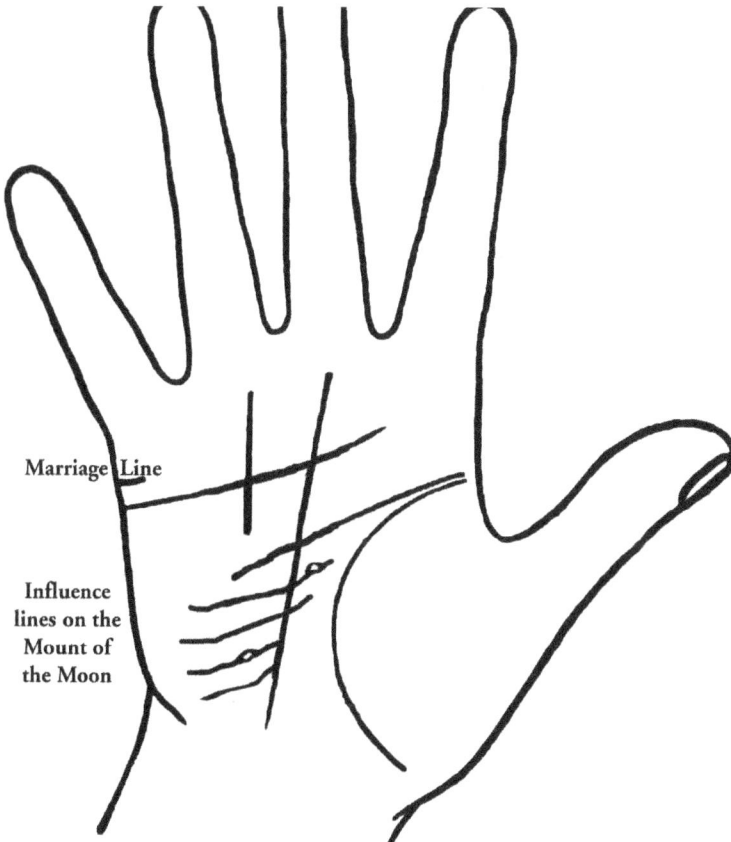

Marriage Line

Influence lines on the Mount of the Moon

Influence lines on the Mount of Venus

These are fine lines that run parallel with the Line of Life, but they must not be confounded with the Line of Mars, or "Sister Life Line," which commences higher up nearer the Mount of Mars.

These Venus Influence Lines are more often found with those persons who have what is called the "Venus temperament," or who are intensely emotional and passionate. When many of such lines are seen, the subject cannot live without love, and will have many "affairs" at the same time.

As such an influence line runs parallel with the Life Line, or turns away from it, so it can be judged how long such an influence will last and with fair accuracy the date when it will occur (see chapter on timing). These influence lines, however, never have the same importance or meaning as those previously ascribed to the Line of Fate.

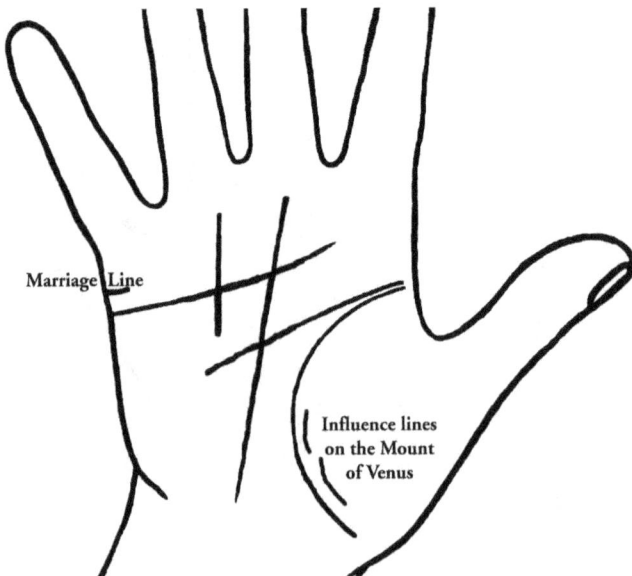

Marriage Line

Influence lines
on the Mount
of Venus

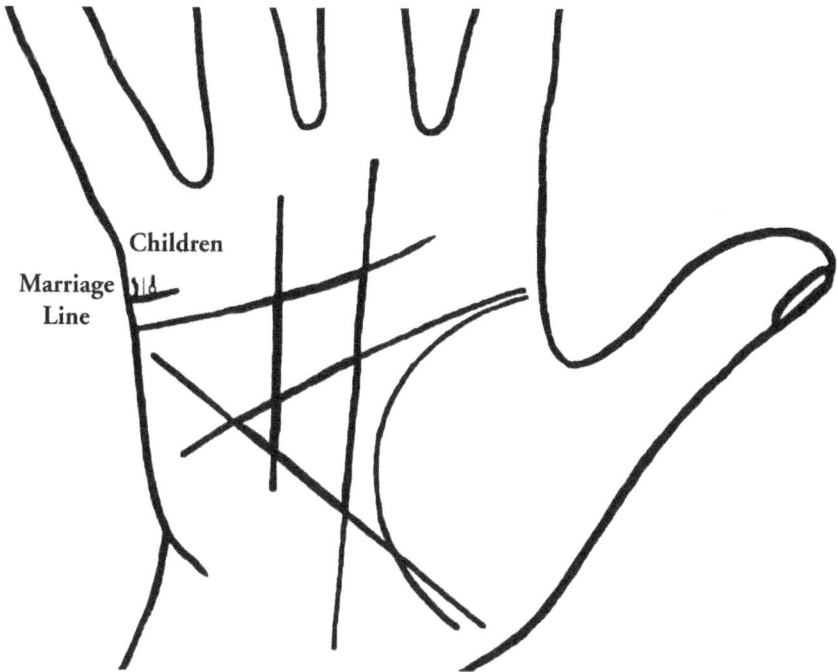

Children

Marriage
Line

Children

The lines relating to children are those finely marked upright lines found immediately above the Line of Marriage. A very good method to see these lines is to press this portion of the hand with the tips of the fingers, and then note which of these small lines stand out the most clearly.

Sometimes they are extremely deeply marked, and as a rule much more so on a woman's hand than on a man's. In many cases it is necessary to employ a magnifying glass in order to see them.

Broad and deep lines denote male children, fine and narrow lines, females.

When they appear as straight lines they denote strong

healthy children, but when very faint or crooked, the children indicated are always delicate.

When the first part of the little line (taking it upward from the Line of Marriage) is marked with a small "island," such a child will be very delicate in its early life, but if the line appears well marked when the "island" is passed, the probability is that it will grow up strong and healthy.

Note: Never predict the ill health or death of anyone.

When one line stands out very clear and distinct among the others, the child the mark indicates will be closest to the parent, and will be more successful than any of the others.

To know the number of children anyone will have, it is necessary to count these lines from the outside of the hand in towards the palm.

A person with the Mount of Venus very flat on the hand, and very poorly developed, is not likely to have any children at all, and this is all the more certain if the first Bracelet is found rising up like an arch into or towards the palm.

11

The Line of Health

Foreshadowing Illness

There has been considerable discussion among students of this subject as to the part of the hand on which the Line of Health commences. My own theory, and one that I have proved by over twenty-five years' experience and also watching its growth on the hands of children, is, that it rises at the base of or on the face of the Mount of Mercury, and as it grows across the hand and attacks the Line of Life, it foreshadows the development of illness.

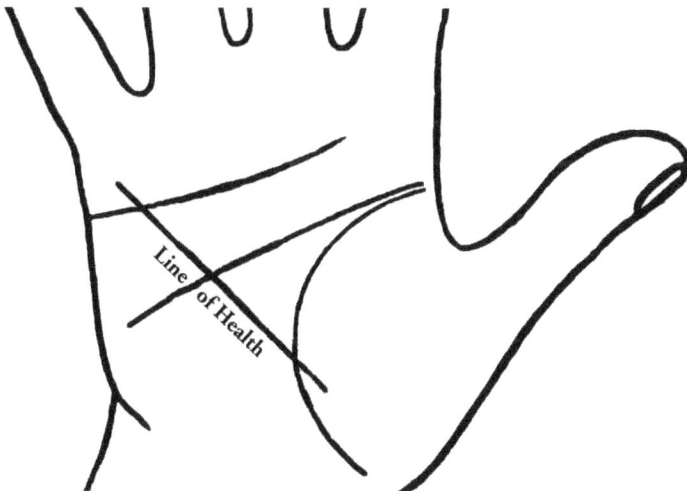

The Line of Life merely relates to the promised length of life from heredity and natural causes, but the Line of Health denotes the effect of the type of life the subject has led. Where these two lines come together, if one is of equal strength to the other, will be a sign of death even if the Line of Life passes this point and appears to be a much greater length.

The Line of Mercury, or of Health, relating as it does to the nervous system, and also to the mind (Mercury), lends itself to the supposition that the all-knowing subconscious brain is cognizant, even at an early age, of the force of resistance in the nervous system. It may know how long this force will last, when it will be exhausted, and consequently may mark the hand long years in advance.

Subject to change

The Line of Health is one of the lines of the hand most subject to changes. It is the thermometer of the life showing its "rise and fall" as the case may be. I have seen this mysterious line look deep and threatening during the early years of a life, and completely fade away as greater health and strength took possession of the body.

Again, I have often seen it look deeper and more ominous as the wear and tear, especially of the nervous system, began to make itself manifest, or when the subject over-taxed his mental strength.

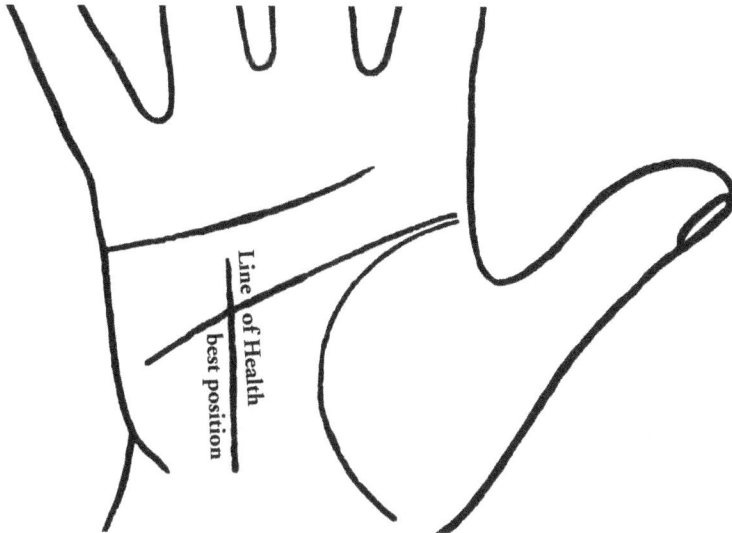

Line of Health best position

An excellent sign

Further, it is an excellent sign to be without this line altogether. Its absence denotes an extremely robust, strong constitution, and a healthy state of the nervous system.

If a hand has the Line of Health, the best position for it is to lie straight down the hand, and not approach or touch the Line of Life. When found crossing the hand, and touching or throwing branches across to the Line of Life, it foretells that there is some illness.

If it rises and seems like a branch from the Heart Line, especially if both these lines are broad in appearance and with the Health Line running down the palm coming in contact with the Line of Life, it indicates a weakness or disease of the heart.

When the finger nails are short, without moons, and round, and the Line of Health is strongly marked, it is a sign that the heart is threatened.

When the nails are long and almond-shaped, there is danger of weakness of the lungs. With the same shape of nails, and with islands in the upper part of the Health Line, diseases of the lungs will manifest.

When this line is very red in small spots, especially when pressed, rheumatic fever is indicated. When twisted, irregular, and yellowish in color, the subject will suffer from liver complaints.

When found heavily marked, and only joining the Heart and Head Lines together, it foreshadows brain disease, especially when any islands are marked on the Line of Head.

The Line of Health, running straight down the hand but not touching the Line of Life, indicates that though the constitution may not be robust, it is wiry, and there is great reserve resistance to disease.

In connection with the examination of the Line of Health, the student must always look for other indications in the rest of the lines of the hand, more especially on the Line of Life and Line of the Head. For instance, when the Line of Life looks very chained and weak, the Health Line on a hand will naturally increase the danger of delicate health; and when found with a Line of the Head full of little islands, or like a chain, such a Health Line more clearly foreshadows brain disease, severe headaches, etc.

By a study of this line the most valuable warnings may be given of approaching ill-health. Whether persons will follow the warnings or not is a question. My experience is that they do not and will not, and therefore, whatever is indicated will most probably come to pass.

Although many signposts and warnings are placed in our paths, human nature is either too blind or too self-confident to notice them until it is too late.

The Great Triangle

The Great Triangle is formed by the lines of Head, Life, and Health. The larger this triangle is, the better the individual's health, because the Line of Health will be further removed from the Life Line. The views of life will also be broader and the field of action less limited.

When the upper angle (made by the Head and Life Lines) is acute, the subject will be more nervous, timid, and sensitive.

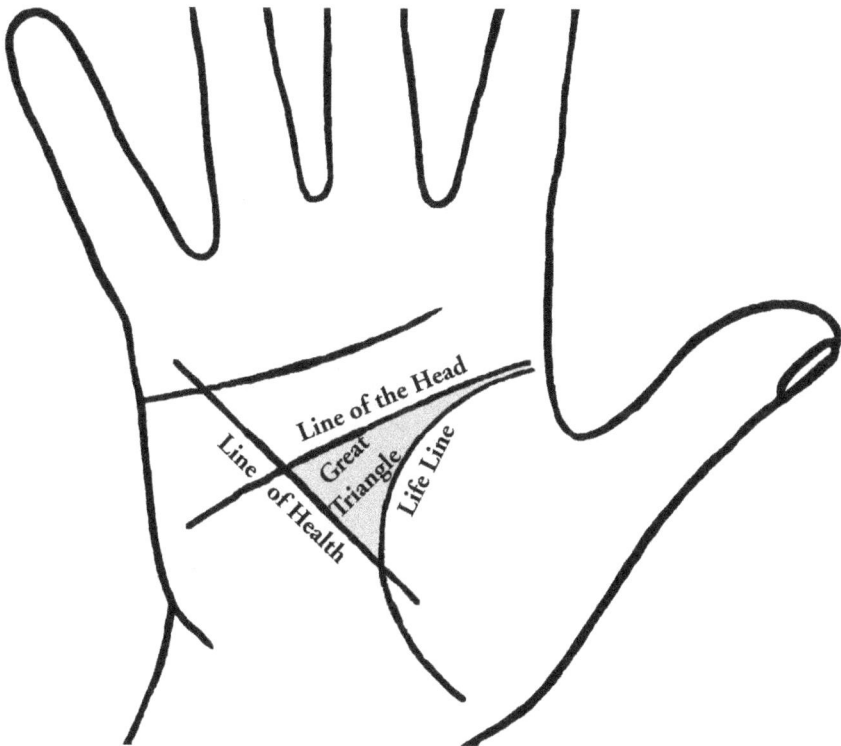

The Quadrangle

The Quadrangle, as its name implies, is that space lying between the Lines of the Head and the Heart.

To be well marked, it should be even in shape and not narrow at either end. When marked in this way it denotes balance of judgment, level-headedness in all things, and is an excellent sign to have.

It represents a person's disposition or mental attitude towards others. When extremely narrow it indicates narrowness of views and bigotry in regard to religion.

When excessively wide, it denotes a lack of judgment in all things and too much looseness of views for one's good.

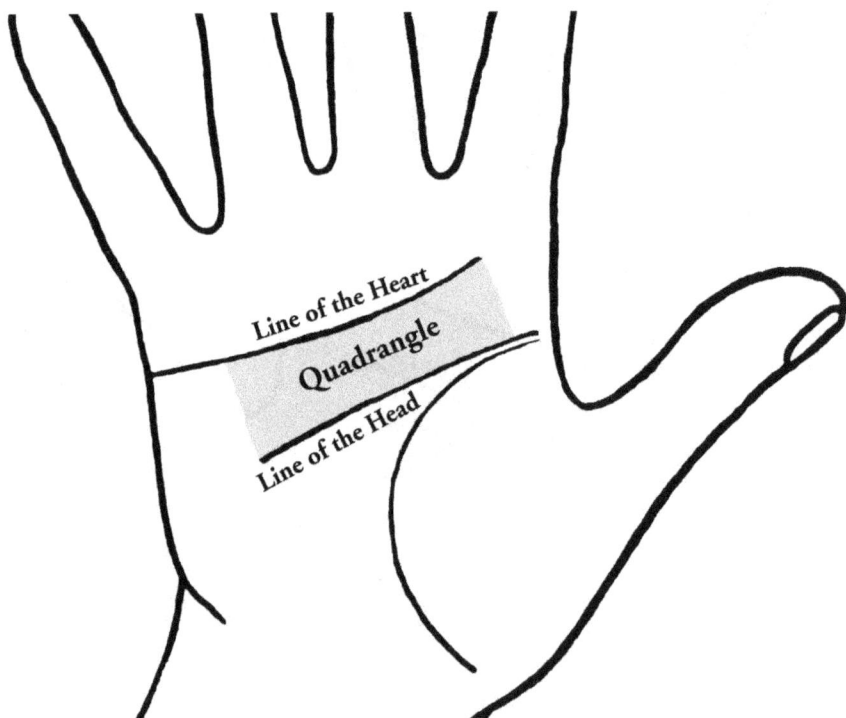

Girdle, Ring, & Bracelets 12

The Girdle of Venus

The Girdle of Venus is that broken or sometimes unbroken kind of semi-circular line that is sometimes found rising from the base of the first finger to the base of the fourth. The Girdle of Venus relates more to the mental side of the symbolism of the Venus nature.

I have found that persons with this sign are more mentally sensual than physically so. They love to read or write books on the subject of sex, but they are not inclined to put their theories and ideas into practice, at least with their own lives.

When broken or made up of little pieces, the Girdle of Venus has little meaning except to show a hysterical temperament. These persons suffer enormously from mood swings, they are very difficult to live with, and when the Girdle of Venus runs off the side of the hand and passes out through the Marriage Lines, their moody, changeable natures generally make marriage for them an unusually unhappy experience.

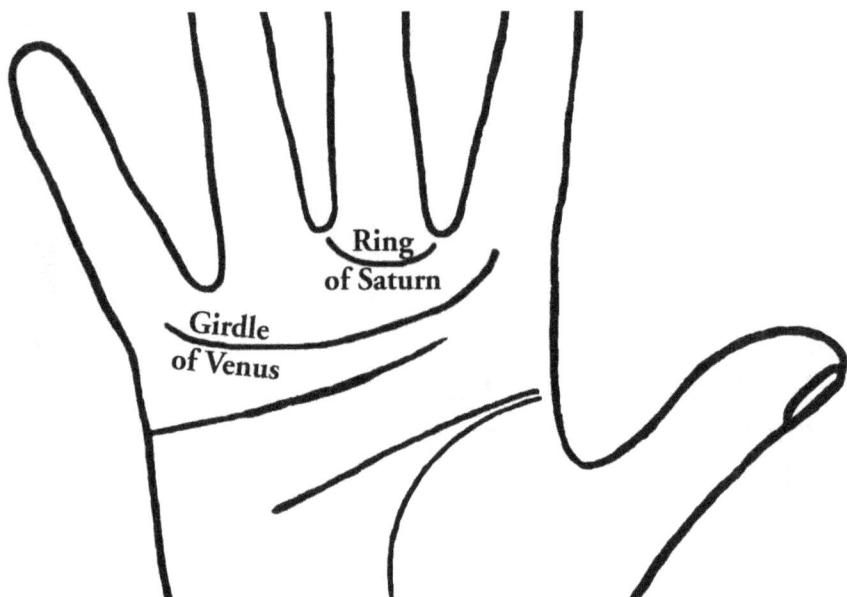

Ring
of Saturn

Girdle
of Venus

The Ring of Saturn

What is called the Ring of Saturn is very seldom found, and it is by no means a good sign to have. It is also a semi-circular line, but found lying across the Mount of Saturn. It is the most unfortunate mark ever to find.

In all my experience I have never been able to come across any person with this mark who succeeded in life or was able to carry any one of their plans to a successful termination. These people seem cut off from their fellow beings in some peculiar and extraordinary way. They are isolated and alone, and they appear to realize their lonely position keenly. They are gloomy, and morbid. They seldom marry, and when they do, it is often a failure.

They are obstinate and headstrong in all their actions; they resent the least advice or interference in their plans. Their lives generally end in suffering, poverty, or by some tragedy or fatality.

The Bracelets

The Bracelets are of very little importance except to throw light on certain points of health. There are supposed to be three of these lines or bracelets at the wrist, which were called by the Greeks the Bracelets of Health, Wealth, and Happiness.

It is very seldom that they can be found together, for experience in life does not give much hope that these three much-sought-after possessions can ever be found together on this side of the grave.

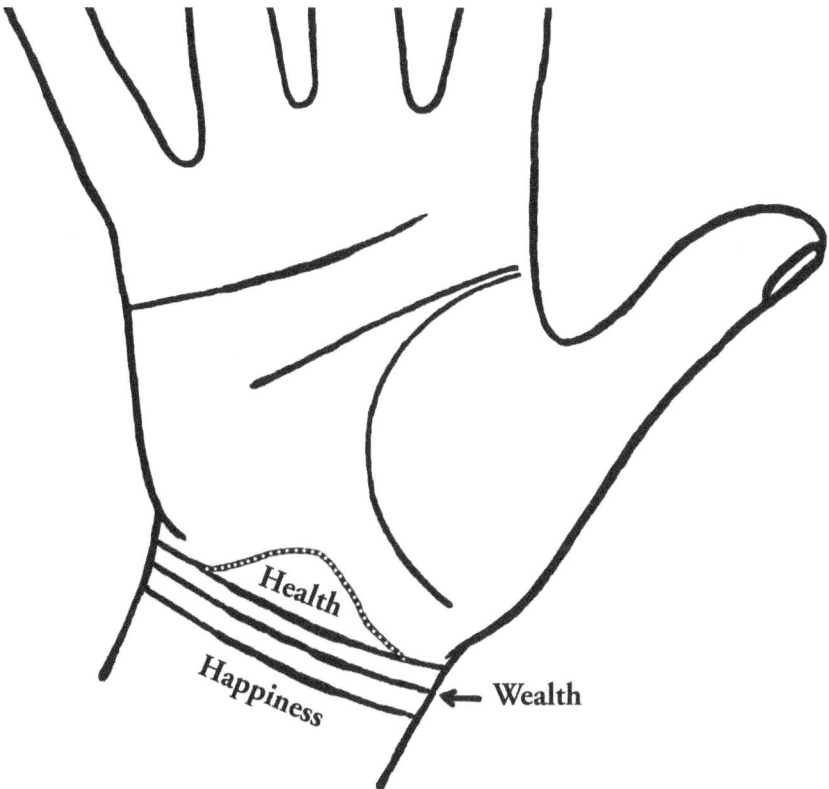

Delving back into the ancient legends of Greece, we find one very significant point in reference to the first bracelet, the one nearest the palm, which represents Health.

Apparently, at one period of the ancient Greek civilization all women had to come to the priest at their Temple to have their hands examined before they were allowed to marry. If the priest found this first Bracelet out of its place and rising up into the hand in the shape of an arch, he would not allow the woman possessing this sign to be married under any circumstance, the idea being that it represented some internal malformation that would prevent her bringing children into the world. In such cases these women were made Vestal Virgins in the temples.

13

Occult Mysteries & Travel

The Line of Intuition

The Line of Intuition is seldom found on other types of hand than those of the Philosophic, the Conic, and the Psychic, but it is sometimes found on the Spatulate.

It takes more or less the formation of a semi-circle from the face of the Mount of Mercury to that of the Mount of the Moon, or may be found on the Mount of the Moon alone. It must not be confused with the Line of Health, but is found as a distinct mark in itself.

It denotes a highly-strung sensitive temperament, along with presentiments, inspiration, clairvoyance of the highest kind, clear vivid dreams which often come to pass, intuition as to how things should be done, and very often manifests itself in inspired speaking and writing of the highest quality.

It is much more often found on women's hands than on men's, although many cases have come under my notice of its being unusually clearly marked on some men's hands. In each case the possessor of it had most remarkable powers

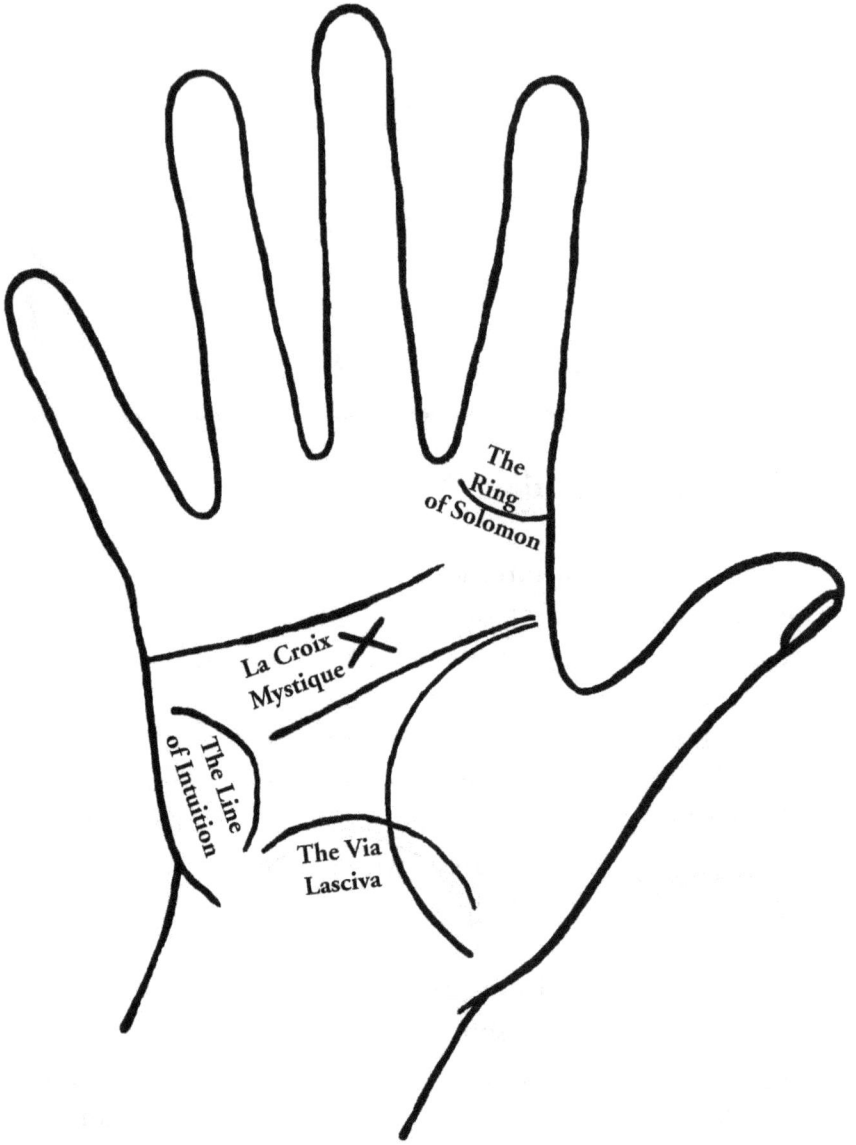

The
Ring
of Solomon

La Croix
Mystique ✕

The Line
of Intuition

The Via
Lasciva

and unusual faculties, as well as the gift of intuition, even concerning purely mundane subjects that in an ordinary state they knew nothing whatever about.

I use the words "ordinary state" advisably here, because such people are not always in the condition of mind when these strange faculties may be employed. Several of these people were absolutely uneducated, and yet at times, when thrown into an inspired state, they were able to explain the most intricate problems with the greatest accuracy. If asked, however, from where they obtained their knowledge, they were only able to reply that "it came to them" when in certain moods.

One man I knew well had such remarkable dreams of coming events that he was able to warn many people weeks and months in advance of dangers that lay before them and his warnings in many cases saved lives.

With all people who were gifted in this way I have noticed that they completely lost their strange powers the moment they indulged in alcohol of any kind.

The Via Lasciva

This is a strange mark which takes the form also somewhat of a semi-circle, but in this case it connects the Mount of the Moon with that of Venus, or it may simply run off the hand from the lower part of the Mount of Luna into the wrist.

The first-mentioned formation indicates unbridled sensuality and passion, and where it cuts through the Line of Life it indicates death, but one usually brought about in connection with the licentiousness that it denotes.

This Line running from the Mount of the Moon into the wrist denotes the most sensual dreams, desires, and imaginings, but, unlike the other class, it is usually only dangerous to the person on whose hand it is found.

In both cases there is a tendency towards the taking of drugs especially when the hand is noted to be soft, full, and flabby. With a firm hard palm the subject usually indulges in excessive drinking, and when drinking seems to have no control whatsoever.

If the Line of the Head is found weak-looking, full of islands and descending downwards on the Mount of the Moon, mental illness will sooner or later affect the whole character and career.

La Croix Mystique

What is called "La Croix Mystique" is found in the quadrangle of the hand between the Lines of Heart and Head. It is more usually found in the centre of this part of the hand, but it may be also found nearer the one side of the quadrangle or the other.

This mark denotes a natural gift or talent for mysticism and occultism of all kinds.

When placed nearer Jupiter, it denotes the employment of these studies more to gratify the subject's own pride or ambition than the following out of such things for their own sake.

When it is in the centre of the quadrangle, across the Line of Fate, or immediately under the Mount of Saturn, such studies become more of a religion or are followed for their own worth and the influence, and the truth of occultism will play a leading role in their career. Most likely the possessor of this mark will follow it as a profession, or will crystallize their research into the form of books.

When this mark lies lower down in the quadrangle, nearer to the Mount of the Moon, the subject will study some form of occultism more from a superstitious standpoint than any other. Nonetheless, they will be likely to succeed in doing so, and influence other people through their studies, and with this latter form they will be more likely to write beautiful mystic poetry with the prophetic note running through it very strongly.

The Ring of Solomon

The Ring of Solomon is also one of these strange marks of mysticism and occultism, but in this latter case, owing probably to the qualities signified by the Mount of Jupiter, its possessor will aim at having the power of a master or an adept in such subjects.

Travel

Travels and voyages may be seen on the hand by the little lines that leave the Line of Life and bend over towards the Mount of the Moon.

When a travel line from the Line of Life ends in a small cross the journey undertaken will end in disappointment. When the Line ends in a square, there will be great danger to the subject on such a journey, but they will escape, as the square is a sign of preservation from danger. When the Line ends in an island, the journey will end in loss.

When a travel line crosses over near or on to the Mount of the Moon and ends in a fork or a circle, there will be great danger in undertaking such a journey.

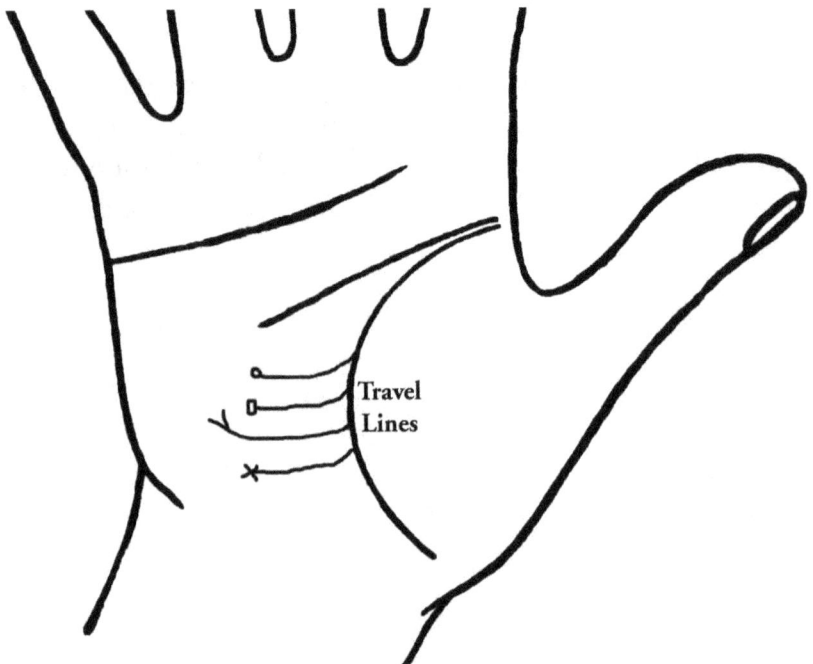

Travel Lines

When, however, the Line of Life itself divides, and one branch of it leans over towards or on to the Mount of the Moon, it denotes that the entire life will be full of change and travel.

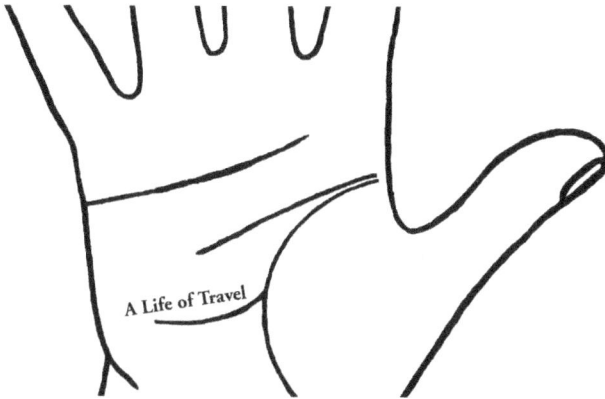

A Life of Travel

If the Line of Life apparently leaves its ordinary course and sweeps over to the Mount of the Moon, the life will be one continual round of travel. The person will settle nowhere, and the end of the life in such a case will take place in some land far distant from their place of birth.

If the Line of Life has no lines or branches leaving it and going in an opposite direction, but keeps to the form of a semi-circle round the Mount of Venus, then such a life will be remarkably free from change and travel, and the person will remain all his life in the land of their birth.

There is always more danger in traveling on water when the subject is found to be born in the following dates:

(1) Between the 21st of June and the 21st of July.
(2) The 21st of October and the 21st of November.
(3) Between the 21st of February and the 21st of March.

There is more likelihood of danger from collision of trains and accidents on land when the subject is born between:

(1) The 21st of April and 21st of May.
(2) The 21st of August and the 21st of September.
(3) The 21st of December and the 21st of January.

Danger from storms, tornadoes, thunder and lightning, is more likely to occur when people are traveling whose birthdays fall between:

(1) The 21st of May and the 21st of June.
(2) The 21st of September and the 21st of October.
(3) The 21st of January and the 21st of February.

Accidents

Accidents are generally marked by lines descending from the Mount of Saturn and touching the Line of Life. When falling on the Line of Head, they increase the danger to the head itself. Descending lines are those that look thicker on the Mount and taper as they come downwards.

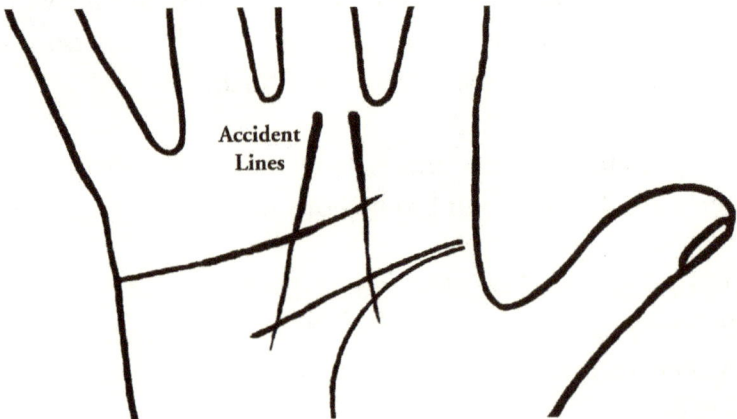

Accident Lines

Other Markings

14

The Island

The Island is never a fortunate sign. Where ever it makes its appearance, it reduces the promise of the line or mount on which it may be found.

On the Line of Life it shows delicacy or illness at that particular date where it appears.

On the Line of Head, weakness of the brain, danger of brain illness.

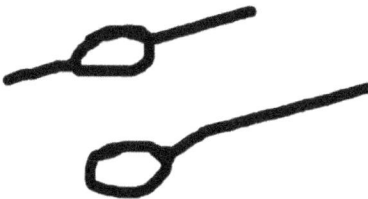

Islands

On the Line of Heart, weakness of the heart, and especially so when under the Mount of the Sun.

On the Line of Fate, heavy loss in worldly matters, worry, and anxiety about the subject's destiny.

On the Line of Sun, loss of position and generally by some scandal.

On the Line of Health, serious illness; if on the upper part of the Line and with small round finger-nails, throat and bronchial troubles. With long nails, diseases of the lungs and chest. With short nails without moons, bad circulation and weak heart; and with very flat nails, nerve diseases.

Lower down on the Line of Health on the Mount of the Moon, it indicates a tendency towards kidney and bladder troubles.

Any line that forms itself into an island or that runs into one, is a bad sign for that line or particular part of the hand on which it is found. An island on any of the mounts weakens the qualities of what the mount expresses.

The Circle

On the Mount of the Sun a circle is favorable, but in all other positions it is unfavorable.

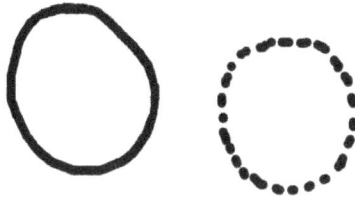

Circles

The Spot

A spot is a sign of a temporary reduction of the qualities of any line on which it may be found.

On the Line of Head, shock or injury. On the Line of Life, sudden illness. On the Line of Health, fever.

On all the other lines spots appear to have less significance.

Spots

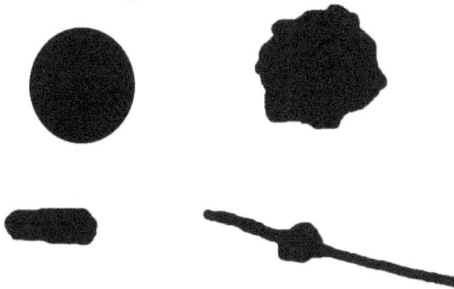

Grilles

The Grille

A grille is very often seen on the mounts of the hand. It denotes difficulties and obstacles in connection with whatever the mount represents, and limited success in whatever quality or talent the mount symbolizes.

The Star

The Star is, with only one exception, a most fortunate mark to possess. On the Mount of Jupiter, the Star promises added honor, power, and position.

On the Mount of Sun, it gives riches and glory, but generally associated with a public life.

On the Mount of Mercury, unusual success in commerce, business, science, or great eloquence, according to other indications of the hand.

On the Mount of Mars under Jupiter, great distinction and celebrity in the military which gives renown, like a Wellington at Waterloo.

Stars

On the Mount of Mars under Mercury, it gives honor won by mentally fighting the battle of life.

On the Mount of the Moon it is a sign of great celebrity arising from the qualities of this mount, through the imagination or creative faculties.

On the Mount of Venus the Star on the centre of this Mount is also a sign of success, but in relation to animal magnetism and sensuality it gives extraordinary success with the opposite sex.

On the Mount of Saturn it is the one unfavorable sign of this particular mark, and on this mount it gives distinction, but one to be dreaded. Such a person will be the plaything of destiny, cast for some terrible part in the tragedy of life. Such a life will end in some terrible disaster, but one which will cause their name to be on everyone's lips. A monarch perhaps, but one crowned by doom.

The Cross

This sign is the direct opposite to the preceding sign, and has only one favorable position, on the Mount of Jupiter where it indicates some extraordinary fortunate affection which will come into the life. On all the other mounts it is bad.

Crosses

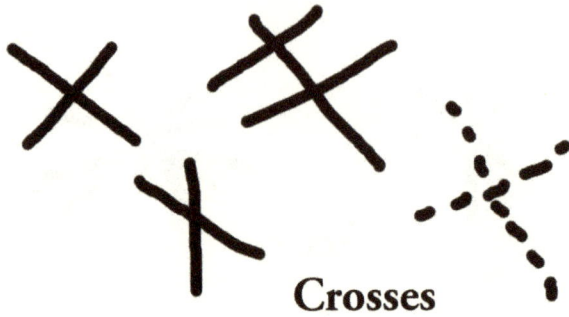

On the Mount of Saturn, violence.

On the Mount of Sun, disappointment in riches.

On the Mount of Mercury, dishonesty.

On the Mount of Mars (under Mercury) great opposition. On the Mount of Mars (under Jupiter) violence and even death from quarrels.

On the Mount of the Moon it denotes the fatal influence of the imagination. Such persons will deceive themselves.

On the Mount of Venus it indicates some fatal influence of the affections.

Above the Line of Head it foretells an accident or injury to the head.

Above the Line of Heart, the sudden death of love.

Squares

The Square

The Square is also called the Mark of Preservation. It shows escape from dangers.

When on the Line of Life it means preservation from death.

On the Line of Fate, preservation from loss, and so on with each quality represented by the different lines.

Are you seeing something bad in a hand?

The first thing to remember is that perhaps you are mistaken. Are you sure that you are seeing a grille? Or could it be a series of squares?

Another thing to remember is that, while the character traits shown on the hands are generally pretty much set, the secondary signs on our hands change as the circumstances around us change.

Do not become frightened based on anything you see in a hand. There is very little that cannot be prevented.

Also, remember never to upset someone by predicting death or serious illness. People are very susceptible to suggestion and you could be setting up a self-fulfilling prophecy.

15

Different Classes of Lines

Color

The lines on the palm should be clearly marked, a good pink or reddish color, and they should be free from breaks, crosses, holes or irregularities of all kinds.

When very pale in color they show lack of strength and loss of energy, and often poor health. When extremely red they indicate excessive energy and a rather violent disposition. When yellow in color they denote a tendency toward liver disease, and indicate a melancholy morose nature.

Forked lines

Forked lines are generally good and increase the quality of the line. For example, at the end of the Line of Head, the fork gives more of what is called a "dual mentality" but less power of concentration on any one subject.

Spots

Spots on a line weaken it and arrest its growth.

Tassels

Tasseled lines are not good signs. They weaken any indication the line itself denotes, and at the end of a Life Line they foreshadow a loss of energy.

Wavy lines

Wavy lines show uncertainty, lack of decision and lack of strength.

Broken lines

Broken lines destroy the meaning of the line at the particular place where the break appears, but if one line starts before the old previous one ends, the break is not so bad and the quality of the line will be continued.

Sister lines

Sister lines increase or double the power of any line, and when lying close together at the Line of the Head, they give it great power and promise.

Islands

Islands are always bad signs and denote weakness or failure of the line or mount on which they may be found.

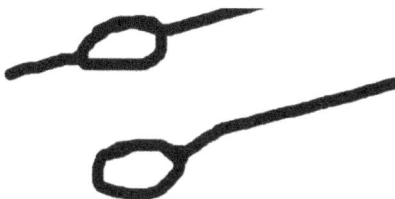

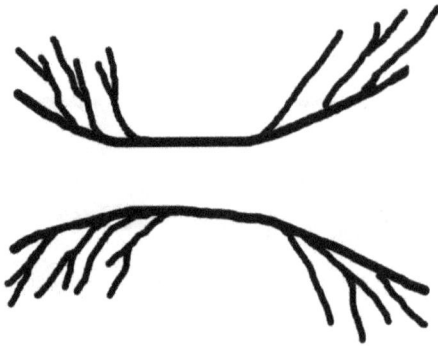

Ascending and descending lines

Ascending lines are good signs for any line from which they start. From the Line of Life they denote increased energy. If they run up to any particular mount or part of the hand, the increased effort or energy will be in that particular direction.

Descending lines are the reverse and mean loss of power.

Chains

Chained lines show lack of strength or purpose.

Worry lines

When the entire hand is covered with a network of small lines, it denotes a highly nervous disposition and usually great worry and lack of decision.

16

Timing

The timing of principal events in the life

The most accurate way in which to tell time by the hand is to divide the Line of Life, the Line of Fate, and the Line of the Head into periods of seven years.

This division into periods of seven is the most natural one of all, as the entire body changes every seven years.

Look for secondary markings such as islands, spots, grilles, stars, crosses, or squares on the three major lines to indicate particular events.

Line of the Head

Under the first finger the period of the life indicated is the first 21 years, the second period contains another section of the three 7's, and lasts until 42 years of age; the third period of 7's which will be found under the third finger indicates the section from 49 to 63, and the fourth section which takes in the remainder of the hand, under the fourth finger, stands for the period from 63 up to the end of life.

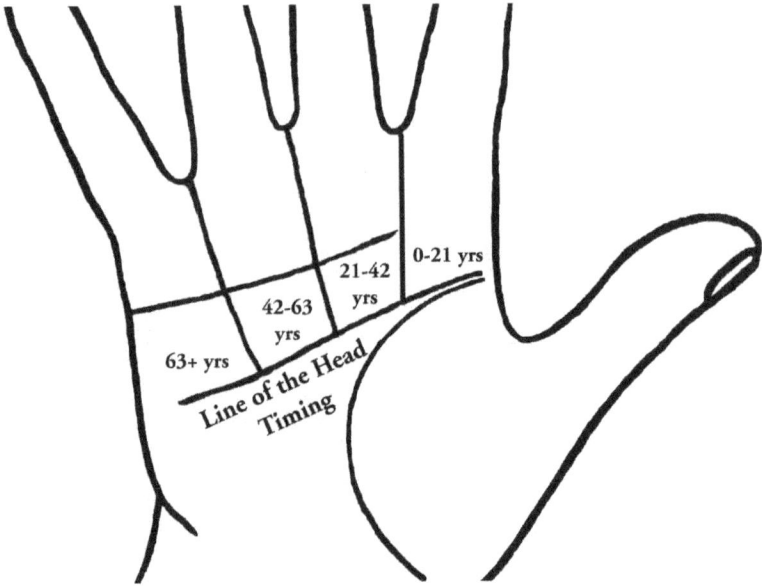

0-21 yrs

21-42 yrs

42-63 yrs

63+ yrs

Line of the Head
Timing

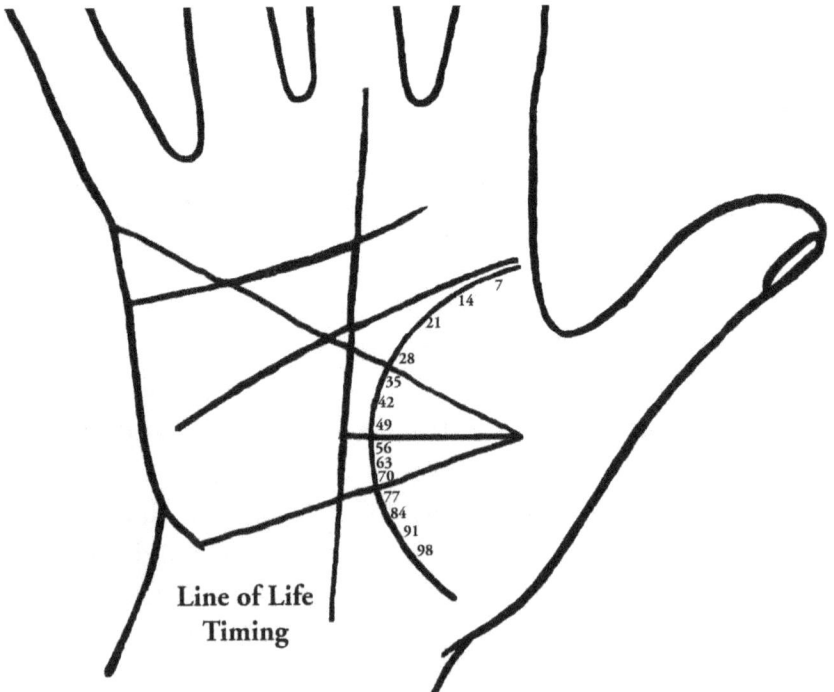

7
14
21
28
35
42
49
56
63
70
77
84
91
98

Line of Life
Timing

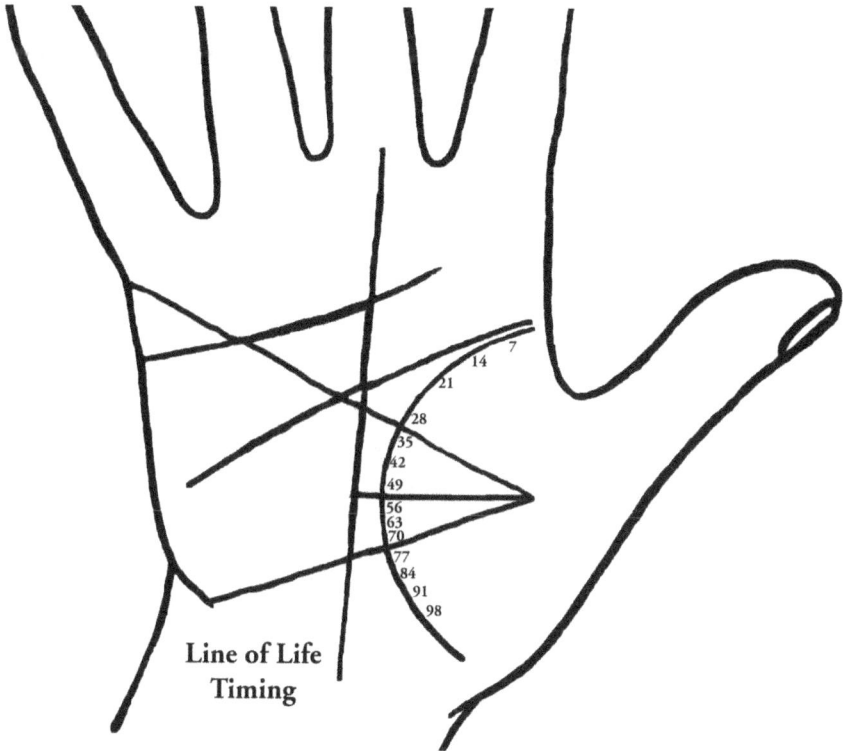

Line of Life
Timing

Ascending Lines

When the Line of Life is found with a number of ascending lines, even if they are small, it denotes a life of greater energy; and the dates at which these lines ascend from the Line of Life may always be considered points at which the subject has made a particular effort towards whatever may have been the special purpose of their destiny at that moment.

When these lines are seen ascending towards or on the Mount of Jupiter, it indicates the desire and ambition to rise in life, especially in some way that would give the subject control or authority over others. If one of the lines is found to be partly arrested or stopped at the Line of the Head, it indicates that the subject has, by some error of judgment, broken or prevented the effort, which started well, from reaching a successful conclusion.

If one of these lines reaches and stops at the Line of Heart, it indicates that the affections have, or will, interfere with the subject's special effort in whatever direction this line indicates.

If one of these lines crosses and joins the Line of Fate, it indicates two distinct dates which are very curious in their meaning. The first date it gives is when this line leaves the Line of Life on its way towards the Line of Fate. The date of this start towards the Line of Fate will be given on the Line of Fate itself, exactly opposite where this line begins to grow from the Line of Life. This mark will denote that the subject has made a determined effort at that moment in his career to make his own destiny, and to break free from the circumstances or people that surround him or tie him down. It is always a successful sign when this line is found to join the Line of Fate, especially if the Line of Fate looks stronger at or about this point of the junction.

The second date is given at the period in the Line of Life when one is reading down the Line of Life itself. The peculiar point about this is that a repetition of circumstances will be found to occur in the destiny. Suppose, for example, one saw this line going towards the Fate Line at twenty-six years of age--a circumstance or repetition of the occurrence will be found to occur at almost double that age, namely, fifty-two years of age, which would give a more or less exact date of this occurrence when reading the Line of Life. As an illustration to help the reader I may say that I have generally found that this mark will indicate that the subject has, in the first instance, broken free from some tie at an early date, and that a similar occurrence will take place at the second date late in life when again the subject seems to break free from some tie, and goes out more into the world for himself.

This curious sign very often helps in deciding matters regarding marriage. The person will apparently assert their independence more, and leave the ties of home life, and again go out in the world and fight the battle for themselves, as they did in the earlier part of their existence, when they probably left their parents' influence and forged ahead for themselves.

When the ascending line is seen crossing over towards the Mount of Saturn, and running as an independent line not joined to the Line of Fate, it will be found that the subject has carried out a kind of second fate. The date when this line left the Line of Life will give the first date of its beginning opposite it on the Fate Line. If the line is a good one it would give its second date when reading down the Line of Life, where, if the line were good, it carried out this second fate to a successful culmination.

The Line of Fate rising from the Line of Life

Another striking and important point is that the date or years marked on the Line of Fate of such a breaking out into the palm, will be found to coincide with the year in the subject's life in which he asserted his independence or launched out into what he more particularly wanted to do. This date will be found to be one of the most important in his career.

A break in the Fate Line is not always a bad sign to have, provided that one side begins before the other ends; in such a case it foretells a complete change in surroundings and position, and if the new line looks good and straight it will be found to mean that the change will bring about an advancement in position commencing at the date when the second line first makes its appearance.

Influence Lines

When any small line joins the Fate Line or goes on with it as an attendant line, such a mark usually indicates marriage at the date when these lines join. If, on the contrary, these lines do not join, marriage with the person is not likely to occur although the affection and influence will be present.

The most important years in a person's life

Although not related to palmistry, I have also made the following curious observation concerning the most important years in people's careers.

People born on the 1st, 10th, 19th, and 28th of any month, and especially in the months of July, August, and January, will find the following years of their lives the most eventful:

1st, 7th, 10th, 16th, 19th, 28th, 34th, 37th, 43rd, 46th, 52nd, 55th, 61st, and 70th.

Those born on the 2nd, 11th, 20th, and 29th of any month, but more especially in July, August, and January, will find the following years of their lives the most eventful:

> 2nd, 7th, 11th, 16th, 20th, 25th, 29th, 34th, 38th, 43rd, 47th, 52nd, 56th, and 70th.

Those born on the 3rd, 12th, 21st, and 30th of any month, but more especially in the months of December and February, will find the following years of their lives the most eventful:

> 3rd, 12th, 21st, 30th, 39th, 48th, 57th, 66th, and 75th.

Those born on the 4th, 13th, 22nd, and 31st, especially in the months of July, August, and January, will find the followings years of their lives the most eventful:

> 1st, 4th, 10th, 13th, 19th, 22nd, 28th, 31st, 37th, 40th, 46th, 49th, 55th, 58th, 64th, 67th, 73rd, and 76th.

Those born on the 5th, 14th, and 23rd of any month, but especially in the months of June and September, will find the following years of their lives the most eventful:

> 5th, 14th, 23rd, 32nd, 41st, 50th, 59th, 68th, and 77th.

Those born on the 6th, 15th, and 24th of any month, but especially in the months of May and October, will find the following years of their lives the most eventful:

> 6th, 15th, 24th, 33rd, 42nd, 51st, 60th, 69th, 78th, and 87th.

Those born on the 7th, 16th, and 25th of any month, especially in the months of July, August, and January, will find the following years of their lives the most eventful:

2nd, 7th, 11th, 16th, 20th, 25th, 29th, 34th, 38th, 43rd, 47th, 56th, 61st, 65th, 70th, 74th, and 79th.

Those born on the 8th, 17th, and 26th of any month, but more especially in the months of January, February, July, and August, will find the following years of their lives the most eventful:

8th, 17th, 26th, 35th, 44th, 53rd, 62nd, 71st, and 80th.

Those born on the 9th, 18th, and 27th of any month, but more especially in the months of April, October, and November, will find the following years of their lives the most eventful:

9th, 18th, 27th, 36th, 45th, 54th, 63rd, 72nd, and 81st.

Index

M

www.learnancientwisdom.com

Other Books of Ancient Wisdom

The Sweat Lodge is For Everyone

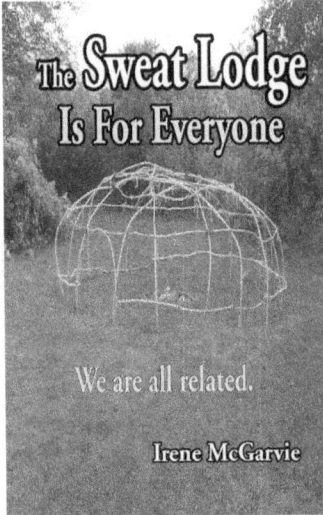

ISBN 978-0-9737470-6-5 $19.95

The Native American Sweat Lodge Ceremony offers so many benefits, both spiritual and physical for anyone who has the opportunity to take part in one.

This book is the non-Native's guide to understanding, participating in, and benefiting from Native American Sweat Lodge ceremonies.

Messages in Your Tea Cup

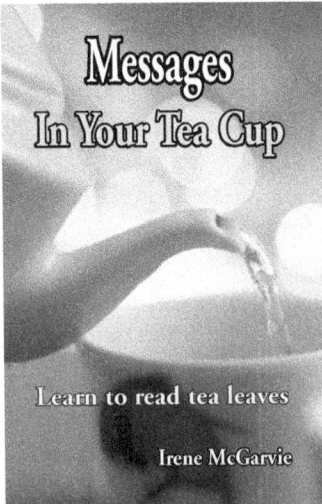

ISBN 978-0-9783939-6-0 $19.95

Have you ever wished that you could predict the future? Throughout history people all over the world have been able to predict future events and get advice from"beyond" through tea leaf reading.

This book will teach you everything that you need to know to begin reading tea leaves immediately.

Other Books of Ancient Wisdom

Séances in Washington

Séances in Washington:

Abraham Lincoln and Spiritualism during the Civil War

Nettie Colburn Maynard

ISBN 978-0-9783939-7-7 $19.95

Abraham Lincoln and Spiritualism during the Civil War.

This book is the first-hand account of the experiences of a Spiritualist medium in Washington during the Civil War. It created tremendous controversy when it was originally published in 1891, but there were enough credible witnesses to confirm her account of events that it could not be disputed.

The Spirituality of Money

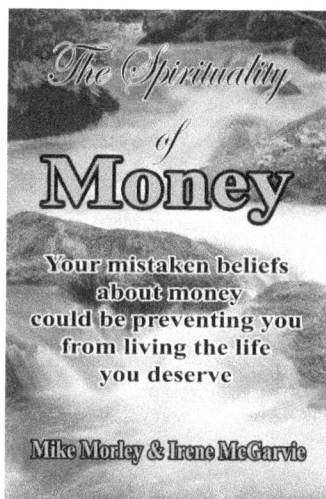

The Spirituality of **Money**

Your mistaken beliefs about money could be preventing you from living the life you deserve

Mike Morley & Irene McGarvie

ISBN 978-0-9783939-3-9 $9.95

Does it feel like money is a constant struggle for you? We keep hearing about how easy it is to "manifest" anything we want, including money, but for most people it just isn't that easy.

This book will help you recognize the false beliefs about money that are preventing you from living the life of affluence and abundance that you deserve.

Other Books of Ancient Wisdom

Mirror Gazing

ISBN 978-1-926826-01-1 $19.95

Mirror Gazing is a technique that enables you to see and interact with the spirits of departed loved ones. Great inventors throughout history have used it as a means of tapping into their creative abilities. For centuries churches have condemned mirror gazing as satanic or evil, and yet many Biblical figures used a form of it to receive Divine guidance. So which is it, a useful skill or a demonic tool? Read this book and decide for yourself.

Help and Advice from the Other Side

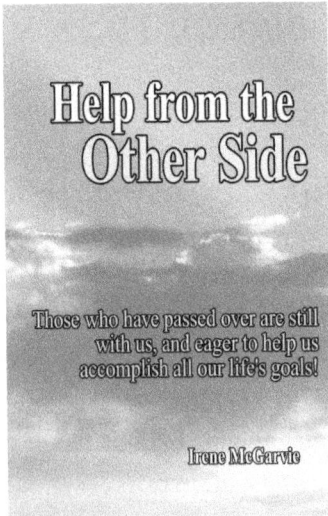

ISBN 978-1-926826-00-4 $19.95

Those who have passed over are still with us, and eager to help us accomplish our life's goals. Learn the techniques used by all the great achievers throughout history to overcome adversity.

Even if we can't see any evidence of it, and **even if we don't believe in it**, we can access all the help and information of the universe, and we can use it to be more successful in all areas of our lives.